501

ways to be a better cross stitcher

501 ways to be a better cross stitcher

Editor:
Amanda Robinson

Art Editor:
Claire Watkins

Words:
Jill Johnson

Production:
Louise Cassell

Editorial Assistant:
Laura Crisp

Illustrations:
Esther Curtis

UK SUBSCRIPTION QUERIES
☎ 01858 438 822
Fax: 01858 461 739
email: origin@subscription.co.uk

USA & CANADA SUBSCRIPTION QUERIES
☎ 1-877 363 1310
Fax: 514 355 3332
email: expsmag@expressmag.com

ALL OTHER OVERSEAS
SUBSCRIPTION QUERIES
☎ 0044 1858 438 822
Fax: 0044 1858 461 739
email: origin@subscription.co.uk

Published by: Kandour Ltd, 1-3 Colebrooke Place, London L1 8HZ

Origin Publishing Ltd, 14th Floor, Tower House, Fairfax Street, Bristol BS1 3BN
☎ 0117 927 9009 Fax: 0117 314 8310

Origin Publishing is dedicated to producing the very best consumer specialist interest magazines - magazines designed to inform our readers, enhance their lives and give them the best value possible. Our newsstand magazines include *The World of Cross Stitching, Cross Stitch Crazy, Cross Stitch Gold, Cross Stitch Card Shop, Card Making & Papercraft, Your Hair, Hair Ideas, 220 Triathlon, Focus and Koi, Ponds & Gardens*

Origin Publishing Ltd is a BBC Worldwide Group company

Dear Reader

We hope you enjoy this fantastic book, free with *The World of Cross Stitching*. Packed with the most comprehensive listing of unmissable tips and advice, '501 ways to be a better cross stitcher' will become an essential part of your sewing workstation - and you won't be able to go anywhere without it!

Bursting with information from a wide range of stitching experts, and broken down into useful categories, if ever you're stuck you'll know where to turn straight away!

Amanda

Amanda Robinson,
Editor

contents

It's a fact   Q&A   Top tips

Beginners' basics

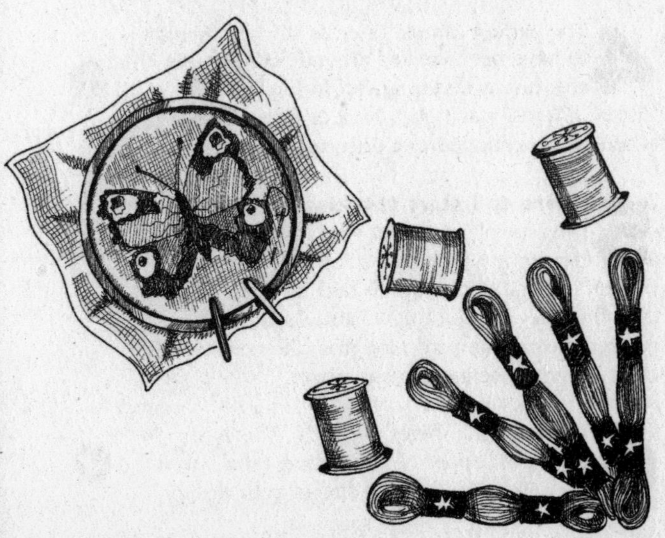

1 Cross stitch is one of the oldest and simplest embroidery stitches and has been used to adorn fabric in almost every part of the world. Its simplicity and versatility have ensured its popularity for many centuries.

2 You can make a design smaller by stitching it on to 18- or 22-count fabric rather than 14. This is useful if you want to use a design that is slightly too big for a card aperture, for example.

3 To calculate the size of a design, divide the number of stitches in both the height and the width by the fabric count. If you have a design 45 stitches wide and 65 stitches high and you are stitching it on 14-count aida, divide 45 by 14 for the width and 65 by 14 for the height. It will measure 3.24x4.6in.

4 The earliest sample of cross stitch is thought to have been created around 500AD - this was discovered in Egypt. In England, the history of cross stitch goes back as far as 679AD where it is mentioned in a document.

5 **Where do I start stitching my design?**
The best place to start stitching a design is at the centre of the chart. Fold your cut piece of fabric in half both ways to find its centre and then find the middle of the chart - usually this is marked clearly. Start stitching from the centre of the chart on to the centre of your fabric.

6 HPI stands for 'holes per inch'. This is an important feature of all stitching fabrics as it determines the finished size of your design.

7 What sort of fabric should I stitch on?

Beginners should use 14-count aida. It is one of the favourite fabrics of stitchers. If you feel you may have trouble seeing the holes, opt for an 11-count fabric until you get used to working the cross stitches, and then move on to 14-count.

8

Cross stitch isn't difficult – with one basic stitch you can complete almost any design you like. It is a fabulous hobby, enjoyed by thousands of people, and enables you to create beautiful pictures and gifts for yourself and others.

9 How do I stop my threads slipping when I try to anchor them at the back?

Make a knot in the end of the thread and push the needle down through the fabric away from the area you are going to be stitching. Bring up the needle at the point you need to stitch and work as normal. The knot will hold the end in place and can be cut off later. This method allows you to position the tail where it will be covered with stitches, securing the thread firmly.

10 Can I carry a thread across the back of my stitching to another area of the same colour?

You can do this, but it's best to limit yourself to a distance of no longer than three or four stitches. Any longer and you may pull the thread too tightly and distort your stitching. It's also not a good idea to carry your thread across an area that is going to remain unstitched, as the thread may be visible through the fabric, showing up as a faint outline that could spoil the finished piece of stitching.

11 People often wonder how to pronounce the word 'aida' – is it 'ada' or 'ayeeda'? We checked up with several manufacturers of fabric and the pronunciation is actually 'ieeda' as in the famous German opera. Aida was an invention of Zweigart, a well-known fabric manufacturer, at the beginning of the 20th century. It referred to the type of fabric - the Aida weave - so everyone uses this name.

12 To avoid making errors with counting, keep counting and keep checking the position of your stitches on the chart. When you are stitching a border, for example, it is easy to make a mistake and miss out a stitch, realising your error when the border doesn't join up! Always stitch the centre of the design first and finish with the border. As you stitch, you can then use the centre of the design to check that your border lines up.

13 **How do I secure a thread firmly?** The best way to anchor your thread firmly in place is to use the first few stitches. When starting off a length, push the needle into the fabric and leave a 5cm tail at the back of the fabric. As you work the first few stitches, hold the 'tail' in place so that the stitches are worked over it and secure it firmly in position.

14 A half cross stitch is half of a whole cross stitch, ie the first arm of the stitch. This is often used by designers to add depth and dimension to cross stitch designs. Half cross stitch should be worked in the direction of the top arm of the whole cross stitches in the design, so that it ties in with the design as a whole.

15 Finish off before you reach the final 5cm (2in) of your thread. You won't find it easy to stitch this close to the end and the thread may also be worn, so your stitching won't look as even and professional.

16 If you are working on a design that has lots of areas where there are two tiny symbols in a single square, divided by a backstitch line, and the symbols are both the same, you need to work the single cross stitch as normal and then divide the stitch with a backstitch to add the detail. The two tiny symbols have been printed in this way so that the backstitch doesn't obscure them, as it may have done if just one large symbol had been used.

17 **What is the 'loop method' of starting off the thread?**

This is a great technique to use if you need to work a single stitch in an area. It can only be used when working with an even number of strands. If the design uses two strands of cotton, fold a single strand of cotton in half and thread the cut ends through the needle to leave the loop hanging. Make the first half of the cross stitch, leaving the loop at the back of the work. As you take the needle back down through the fabric, pass the needle and thread through the loop and pull firmly to secure the thread in place.

18 The easiest ways to buy stitching materials are from needlecraft stores and by mail order. It is also becoming increasingly popular to order over the internet. Just make sure you are ordering from a secure site.

19 If you are using a hoop, you will find the 'stabbing method' the best way to stitch. This keeps your stitches looking beautifully neat. Take the needle straight down through the fabric and then straight back up through the next hole, so that you are performing two separate movements. You should find that you get into a rhythm as you stitch.

20 **Which fabric is best for projects using fractional stitches?**
It is easiest to work fractional stitches on an evenweave fabric because evenweave naturally provides a central hole for working a quarter stitch. If you are working on aida fabric you will need to pierce the centre of the aida block using a small crewel needle and this can sometimes cause the fractional stitch to look messy.

21 **What is the best way to remove creases from aida fabric?**
If pressing the fabric alone won't remove the stubborn creases, rinse the fabric thoroughly in warm water until it becomes flexible. Then roll it up in a soft clean towel until it is just damp. Finally, press the damp fabric and this should remove all the creases.

22 Aida is available in a huge range of shades, so there is something suitable for everyone. Choose from bright colours for Christmas stitching, wonderful shades for spring, rustic colours for samplers and a great range of neutral colours suitable for many different styles of project.

23 **How do I finish off my thread?** Finish off your thread neatly by running your needle through the back of two or three stitches you have already worked. Then, snip the ends close to the fabric. Get into the habit of finishing neatly like this right from the start and you'll find your stitching looks more professional and is easier to mount and frame.

24 When you first pick a cross stitch project, choose a design that you really like and not one that someone has 'convinced' you is a great idea. There is little point in stitching something if you won't like it when it's finished. Although you could give it away...

25 Try and make sure that the first design you stitch isn't too complicated. It should only contain a small number of colours and just whole stitch and backstitch. This will enable you to complete the design quickly. You will soon be able to move to more complicated projects when you have become familiar with all the basics.

26 Aida is sized by 'count' – the number of blocks of stitching per inch (2.5cm) of fabric. It is widely available in various sizes from 11- through to 20-count, with the most popular size being 14-count. This is the count of fabric that is recommended in most magazines and on a lot of standard charts that you can buy. It is probably the best count aida to start stitching on. The higher the count, the finer your stitching will become and the greater will be your need for a good magnifying glass!

27 'Stitching over two' is a term used when stitching on evenweave fabric. Generally, this will be a 28-count evenweave and each stitch is worked over two threads of the fabric to give a stitch that's the same size as it would be if worked on 14-count aida.

28 When stitching designs on fabric to mount into ready-made accessories (handbag mirrors, coasters) keep the back of your stitching as neat as possible. Snip off any thread ends close to the fabric and never use knots to secure threads in place. This will ensure the back of your stitching isn't too bulky and that backplates, for example, will clip easily in place.

29 To keep stitching neat, make all your cross stitches face the same way. Think also about how you handle the thread. To make the strands lie evenly on top of the fabric you need to pull out the strands one by one and then smooth them together to thread the needle. Try to keep your tension even too by pulling the thread taut but not too tight.

30 **What are fractional stitches?** Fractional stitches are a modified cross stitch and they are used by designers to make some shapes and outlines look more natural. Look out for half, three-quarter and quarter stitches. Half cross stitch is usually given a separate symbol in the key, whereas three-quarter and quarter are usually shown on the chart by a smaller version of the cross stitch symbol, positioned in the corner of a square.

31 For medium to large projects, or designs that are going to take a long while to stitch, take the time to bind the fabric around the edges to prevent it from fraying. However, if you are working on a smaller design, such as a quick picture or card, you don't need to bind the fabric then as it is only going to take a few hours or evenings to stitch.

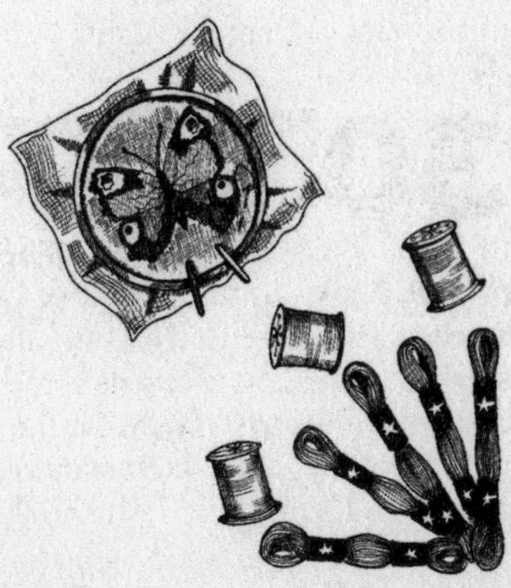

Beads, buttons & charms

32 Beads come in all sorts of different finishes, whether you want matt, sparkly, antique etc. Visit your local needlecraft stockist to see some of the wide range available for you to use.

33 There are tubular beads, hexagonal beads, triangular ones and square, as well as more unusual shapes such as hearts and teardrops. Experiment with a selection of beads to see which shapes work best on different designs.

34 **What colour thread should I use to add beads to a design?**
This depends on the colour of the bead you are using. If the bead is transparent, then use a colour of thread that will merge into the background fabric. However, if the bead is opaque, try and match the thread colour as closely as possible to that of the bead.

35 The correct size beads for the fabric you are working on are:
1-2mm (petit) 16/18-count fabric;
3mm (seed) 12/14-count fabric; 4mm 10/11-count fabric; 5mm 8-count fabric; 6mm 6-count fabric.

36 Sometimes you might find that buttons can look rather pulled in when stitched flat against the cross stitch. Making a small thread 'neck' under the button helps to bring it up to the same level as the stitching.

37 When you are adding beads to your stitching, only ever apply one bead with every cross stitch.

38 Brass charms will tarnish over the years, so if you are attaching them to an heirloom design it is a good idea to paint them with a clear glaze. This will prevent them from tarnishing and, in turn, from damaging the fabric and other stitches.

39 Always add your beads last, otherwise your threads will catch round them as you stitch.

40 Don't be tempted to sew a button on too tightly, or the fabric will pucker and your design will be spoilt.

41 **How do I use beads, buttons and charms in a cross stitch design?**
If you enjoy being creative, you will be inspired by some of the wonderful buttons, beads and charms available. You can combine your chosen embellishment with an existing chart, changing a few colours, or even leaving out part of the chart if necessary. Embellishments can be added to any design; whether it is a last-minute card or an heirloom piece.

42 Use a bead as an alternative to a French knot if you aren't confident about stitching them.

43 Invest in a beading needle – a shorter one is easier to stitch beads on to your stitching with.

44 Keep your beads in a small pot or saucer so that they are easy to pick up on the end of the needle as you stitch.

45 What is a good, non-fancy bead to add to a design?

Generally, if you are stitching from a chart, the type of bead used in the original stitched piece should be specified in the key. However, as a general rule, opaque and lined beads, which don't let the light through, work best on darker fabrics, while transparent beads, and other light-reflective finishes, will be overpowered on dark backgrounds and look best on lighter fabrics.

46 Where can I buy beading needles?

Your local needlecraft store should be able to supply or give you details of your nearest stockist or mail order supplier.

47 To iron stitching when you've added beads, set your iron to a cool setting and place the stitched piece face down on a clean fluffy towel. Gently iron the stitching. The beads will be 'absorbed' by the towel, so they won't get damaged or spoil your stitching.

48 What colour thread should I use to attach a charm?

You should always try and match the colour of the thread to the charm or the background fabric, so that it becomes almost invisible once the design is complete.

49 If a bead is uneven and difficult to stitch with you may be using cheap beads. Always buy the best you can afford to ensure the beads are good quality. Then they should be regular sized with even holes, making them easier to use.

50 I have stitched a design with beads - how do I frame it without damaging them?

If you want to use glass in the design, you will need to use a double, or even a triple mount. This will raise the glass away from the fabric. If, however, there is no room around the picture for a mount, you will need to ask a framer to fit spacers between the glass and the cross stitching.

51

Adding a small charm or button to a simple design can make it look really special. Choose an embellishment that fits in with the theme of the design or the colours incorporated in the stitched design.

52 How do I match beads to a design?

One of the simplest ways to introduce beads into a cross stitch design is to substitute one or two of the key colours with beads. If you are using DMC threads you will find that they have cleverly matched the beads in their range to many of its stranded cotton shades. Try stitching holly berries using a bright red bead, or using beads to highlight the centre of a flower. Small areas of beading can really bring a new dimension to your stitching.

Cards

53 Double-sided tape is best for sticking stitching into a card mount – it doesn't make the mess that glue does.

54 **My design looks too small in the card aperture – what can I do?** If you feel that there is too large a margin around the design, try adding some wording to the design using backstitch. This will fill the gap as well as make the card more personal to the occasion for which it is being sent.

55 Two-fold cards are the most suitable for cross stitch. This type of card has three panels with an aperture in the centre panel. The stitching is fitted behind the aperture and the right-hand flap then folds over to cover the back of the stitching.

56 Wadding is added to the back of a design being mounted in a card to gently push the stitches out, giving a more three-dimensional look to the stitching.

57 To make a plain card look more interesting, add a bow or decorate the card in some way. A thin, coloured or metallic line drawn around the aperture can make all the difference to the final appearance of a card.

58 If you are using a dark-coloured card mount you may find that the card shows up through the holes in the stitching. Solve this problem by inserting a piece of white paper behind the stitching to prevent the colour of the card from spoiling your design.

59 How do I choose the right coloured card mount?

Choosing the colour of a card mount is similar to choosing the mount for a picture. Some colours will enhance the stitching whereas others will not do anything for it. For every card there are several alternatives that could be quite suitable, but, in the end, the choice of colour is personal.

60 Brightly-coloured designs often look best in another bright, contrasting colour, but the safest option is to pick one of the thread colours in the design, or, alternatively, choose a colour which contrasts with or complements the fabric and threads.

61 How do I stitch a design to fit a novelty aperture?

It may not be possible to find a chart for some of the more unusual novelty apertures available, but it's easy to design one yourself. Select a sheet of graph paper in a count to match the fabric and tuck this behind the card aperture. Line up the squares so that they are level and then draw round the aperture. You will now be left with a template of the design on the graph paper, which you can colour in and work out a key for the cross stitch design.

62 Don't use the flat surface of a table to mount your designs, as the pins may spoil your furniture. Instead, try and use a surface that is slightly cushioned – a mouse mat is ideal, or you can buy a specialist cutting mat from art shops.

63 **How do I add wadding to a design?** Cut a piece of 2oz wadding to the same shape as the card aperture. After you have positioned and secured the stitching in the card, stick the wadding in place behind the stitching using small pieces of double-sided tape. Then fold down the card flap as normal.

64 A novelty apertured card is one where the aperture has a more unusual shape. There are lots of different apertures available from card companies, including designs for Christmas, weddings and all sorts of other occasions. The apertures can be in the shape of Christmas tree, stockings, bells, hearts or even elaborate floral designs.

65 If your writing lets you down, buy a pre-printed card insert to go inside your stitched card. They're available from card companies and can be printed with a variety of messages, such as 'Best Wishes', 'Season's Greetings' etc. You can then simply add your signature underneath the written message, as you would with a shop-bought card.

66 If you are mounting some stitching in a card for a child, try and make something really special for them by decorating the card with their favourite character, such as Winnie the Pooh, or one from a comic, or pick a coloured card that matches the bold primary colours or pastel shades of their bedroom.

67 Be adventurous. Try using cards that have different finishes such as silver, pearlised, speckled or rough.

68 If you are mounting a small design for a child in a small card or gift tag, why not attach a safety pin to the back of it and they can wear it as a badge too? This is particularly good if the stitching is of their favourite character, such as Tigger or Mickey Mouse.

69 I need to mount some stitching for a teenager – what style of card can you suggest that would be trendy?

Silver is a good colour for teens, giving a modern metallic theme. Cards are also available in corrugated finishes, which gives them a funky, up-to-date feel, too.

Lettering

70 If you rummage through bargain boxes of old charts in stitching shops you will often find alphabet charts marked down in price. These are well worth buying and adding to your library of designs.

71 When adding lettering to a design make sure you have checked your spacing a couple of times before you actually start to stitch. It's better to spend extra time beforehand rather than having to unpick lots of backstitch.

72 Alphabets are great for adding a personal touch to anything. Add a single initial to a pillowcase, towels or napkins. An initial is quick to stitch and looks great mounted in a handbag mirror, powder compact or trinket box to make a speedy but special gift.

73 **How do I work out how much space the lettering will take on a design?** You need to take time to work this out properly. Plot the lettering on a piece of graph paper, allowing spaces between letters and words where necessary. When you are happy with how it looks, count up the number of squares you have used on the graph paper and divide by two to find the centre of your wording. Mark this point on the graph paper. To position your wording centrally on the design, start stitching from the middle of the design from the middle point of your wording. Your lettering should be perfectly balanced.

74 Lettering stitched in colour other than black will not look as harsh – perfect if you want to create a subtle effect.

75 I need to fit a long word in a small space - what is the best type of lettering to use?

Try using an italic style of lettering as the letters can usually be fitted much closer together than an upright alphabet, because of the angle of the letters.

76 When spacing italic letters, some of the letters won't joint up without being too close to the next letter. What can I do about this?

Space italic letters as you would any other letter, leaving at least one square of graph paper between the main bodies of the letters. If the tail doesn't join up with adjacent letters add a few extra stitches to the end of the charted version, so that it resembles joined up writing.

77

Pick out all alphabets that you see in magazines and keep them in a folder. When you need an alphabet to add lettering to a card, or an alphabet to a sampler, you will have a selection of styles to choose from.

78 How can I stop the lettering on my designs from looking messy?

Always add the lettering to your design using a hoop, even if you don't normally use one. This will keep the fabric taut as you stitch and ensure that each stitch lies snug and flat on top of the fabric.

79

If you are adding wording in capital letters and find that you are short of space, change to lower case and you will find you have more room.

80 How many strands should I use to add lettering to a design?
If you are working from a chart it will tell you in the key how many strands you need to use. However, when creating your own design, it will be worth experimenting. On some designs two strands look rather thick, while on others, one strand can sometimes look a little spidery.

81 I want to stitch a short poem I read in a book on to a sampler – is that ok for me to do?
If the poem you choose is only going to be displayed in your own home, (if you're not going to sell your stitching), it absolutely ok.

82 When I stitch lettering it seems to 'pucker' the fabric a little. What am I doing wrong?
You should have your stitching in a frame or hoop, stretched at an even tension. This will ensure that your backstitch in your lettering is flat and even.

83 Use your computer to help you create any lettering you need for your stitching, such as on a sampler. You can at the very least create grids on your computer to print out so that you can fill in squares and space your lettering. Design software is also available that will help you create designs, including doing your own lettering.

84 If you enjoy lettering, why not have a go at blackwork as this involves lots of linework in dark thread as well and creates beautiful designs.

85 If you want to create an attractive alphabet to use in your stitching, invest in a nice fountain pen or calligraphy pen. Sketch your alphabet on graph paper and it should flow more easily using these pens.

86 Stitching an entire alphabet in a rectangle makes an attractive sampler if enclosed in an appropriate border with colourful matching motifs. If you want to try this, the key is to get your spacing right, so carefully plan how your alphabet would fit in rows in a rectangle of fabric by using graph paper.

Equipment & storage

87 You need just five basic pieces of equipment to start stitching: 14-count aida fabric, a small wooden hoop, a pack of size 24 tapestry needles, a skein of stranded cotton and a pair of scissors.

88 **What is a spring tension hoop?** This lightweight hoop is used by many stitchers. It was originally designed for machine embroidery, but the constant and uniform tension it provides makes it ideal for using with cross stitch. The inner hoop can spring out unexpectedly when you are putting your fabric in, so a little care is needed when you are removing the hoop or clipping it in to place.

89 The most commonly used needles for cross stitch are size 24 and 26 tapestry needles. Keep a pack of each of these sizes and you will generally find that one of these is required for your stitching project.

90 A tape measure is a worthwhile addition to any cross stitcher's range of accessories. You will need it for cutting out fabric and measuring frames and card mounts. You can also use it to check the count size of fabric by checking how many holes per inch there are.

91 One of the best ways to store large projects when not working on them is to roll them up and slide them into a long cardboard tube – the sort that you get with rolls of Christmas or birthday paper are ideal. Storing your fabric this way ensures that it is not only kept clean, but will be free from creases, too.

92 Chart markers are very useful if you are stitching a large design. They are a clear window, with a red border, which can be positioned on the area of the chart you are working on. They can be re-used time and again, enabling you to move them around on the chart and follow where you are more easily, so you won't lose your place or miss any stitches.

93 **What should I look for in a pair of embroidery scissors?**
Buy the pair that suits you and then don't lend them to anyone! There are many classic styles of scissors – stork, chanticleer or lion's tail – all of which have been beautifully shaped and look very good in your workbox. However, although these ornamental scissors look beautiful, and many people enjoy using them, practicality should be your main concern. Many people prefer to use plastic-handled scissors or a pair with a wide bow – great if your fingers are a little larger.

94 All embroidery scissors are designed for snipping threads and should last a lifetime if used correctly. Remember to keep them in your workbox and don't use them for cutting any other materials.

95 **Why is it recommended to use a daylight bulb?**
Although a daylight bulb looks like a normal tungsten bulb, it is moulded in blue glass, which filters out the yellow light. This makes it possible to view the colours in a more natural light, essential when stitching a design with lots of different colours or shading. Your eyes will get less tired and strained, so you can do more stitching!

96 **What is Iron on Vilene?**
This is a material that can be bought in stitching shops and haberdashery departments. It is used for backing cross stitch designs to stop fraying and make them easier to handle when mounting. Generally it is used for small items such as designs for handbag mirrors, coasters and keyrings.

97 If you have a magnifier that you use with your stitching, remember that it must always be kept away from direct sunlight as it could be a fire hazard. Some magnifiers come with a cover for this reason, but why not make your own, with a cross stitch design added to it, of course!

98 **Do I need a magnifier as well as a stitching lamp?**
It really depends on your eyesight. If you find it difficult to see the holes in a 14-count fabric, you may well need one, but first, visit your optician to check if you need glasses.

99 The easiest way to record all the threads in a collection is to simply type a list of thread numbers and add to it, but if you buy a colour chart from the manufacturer you will be able to see at a glance exactly which colours you have. Highlight the number of the thread each time you add one to your collection.

100 Store beads, buttons, charms and any other small bits and bobs in empty film canisters.

101 Buying bobbins and project cards makes the task of sorting and storing threads quick and easy, but it is perfectly possible to do this on a budget by using homemade thread organisers and bobbins.

102 **What sort of designs works best in roller frames?**
Roller frames are particularly suited to rectangular shaped designs such as samplers. They help keep the tension even as you stitch and enable you to roll up a completed section of your design without damaging the stitching. Work can be left on a roller frame in between stitching sessions without any danger of the stitching being marked by the frame. Small frames can be held in your hand, but larger frames work best when they are clamped in a floor frame.

103 **Which system is the best to use for organising threads?**
Whether you decide to use master cards, bobbins or simply store the skeins in a box, it is the organisation and tidiness of the threads which is important. A tangled mass of threads makes it difficult to find what you are looking for and the constant handling required to find a particular colour will cause the threads to go fluffy and lose their sheen.

104 When you're new to stitching you don't need much equipment to get started. This makes cross stitch a relatively low-cost hobby and one that is also easily portable. You can build up more equipment as time goes by if you want extra accessories.

105 If you find it difficult to work out how much fabric you need, try using a clever little gadget made by LoRan. It helps you work out exactly how much fabric you need for the design you are stitching. You simply turn the wheel to the appropriate stitch count to find out what size the design will be on a wide range of fabric counts.

106 A thread organiser is a piece of card that is often included in a cross stitch kit. It has a row of holes punched down one side to which you can attach the threads, and then label them with the appropriate symbol for each different-coloured thread. It is easy to make your own from card, too.

107 It is important to store threads correctly because although it might be tempting to keep your threads in a plastic bag, this way will cause them to become quickly tangled and, in time, they will lose their bands, so you won't know what colour you've got. Also, as the threads rub together they will loose some of their sheen and this, in turn, will affect the quality of your stitching.

108 Look after your charts if there is a chance you might want to use them again. There are lots of great stationery products that you can use to keep them clean and uncreased. Create a folder with plastic see-through sleeves and slide the charts in. You can put them in sections alphabetically or in categories such as flowers or animals, so that you can find a chart quickly if you want it.

109 DIY stores are great sources for storage units. Something that has lots of little drawers that your husband might buy to put screws, nails and washers in would be great for you to store beads, buttons, charms, needle packets etc. in.

110 I want a magnifying glass to stitch with as my eyes get tired but I don't want a big one – what can I try as an alternative?

You can get magnifying lenses that clip over glasses or act as glasses – many people find these comfortable to use.

Techniques & stitches

111 Petit point is a technique often used for creating extra detail in a design, particularly for faces. When you work petit point you simply make small half stitches over one strand of the evenweave fabric. All stitches should point in the same direction. Petit point should not be worked on aida, because you would have to pierce the fabric for each stitch, which looks untidy.

112 Chain stitch is occasionally seen in cross stitch designs such as band samplers, where other stitches are incorporated into the design.

113 Iron lightweight interfacing to the reverse side of a design before adding any backstitch lettering. This will prevent any thread that runs between the letters showing through on to the right side.

114 The best way to keep track of complicated backstitch is to use a felt tip pen or colouring pencil to actually draw along the lines on the chart as you stitch them. Doing this will enable you to see at a glance which backstitch lines have been completed and which still need stitching.

115 **What fabric is best for blackwork stitching?**
Blackwork can be stitched on any evenweave fabric. Beginners may prefer to use aida as it is easier to count, but large designs look better on evenweave, such as Jobelan or Linda. The weave on these is much more distinct that on some more traditional linens, making counting easier.

116 The Danish method is where the cross stitch is worked in rows, working a row of half cross stitch and then completing the top arm on the return journey.

117 **What sort of stitch is used on silk gauze?**
As silk gauze is too fine to stitch whole cross stitch on it, half cross stitch is used instead. The needle is brought out at the bottom left-hand corner and taken back down through the top right-hand corner of a square. Just a single strand of cotton or silk is needed, threaded through a size 28 tapestry needle.

118 Rice stitch is a variation on simple cross stitch. On a large-holed fabric it gives the appearance of dense cover, because the reverse side stitching shows through more. It is often worked in two colours, one for the large crosses and another shade for the small stitches. Make the large crosses first, adding the smaller ones afterwards.

119 Lazy daisy stitch is often incorporated into cross stitch designs as it is useful for showing the petals of flowers or other details and is simple to learn with a little practice on some spare fabric.

120 Blackwork originated in the Middle East, in Muslim communities where the teaching of the Koran forbade figurative designs. It was introduced to Europe through Spain and is mentioned in Chaucer's *Canterbury Tales*. It became popular in Tudor times and is shown in many paintings of that period.

121 What is the difference between backstitch and long stitch? Backstitch is used to outline parts of a design. It follows the same chart grid as cross stitch with each stitch moving up, along, or diagonally across one square at a time. It is worked in a backward circular motion and is added after the cross stitch. Long stitch is a more free form technique. Like backstitch it is also usually added at the end and is used to show flower stems, the spokes of a wheel or an animal's whiskers, for instance. It consists of a very long stitch, which lies across the front of the cross stitch and can span the length of many cross stitches at once.

122 Colonial knots are easier to stitch than French knots, so try one if a French knot is shown on a chart.

123 An Algerian eye is a striking decorative stitch that is created from a series of stitches all radiating out of the same central hole. It is easy to increase the size of your Algerian eye if you want to. Try working 12 stitches instead of eight and covering a nine-square grid.

124 Blackwork is embroidery worked in black thread. At first glance it looks completely different to cross stitch, but both techniques are classed as counted thread embroidery, worked on evenweave fabric.

125 Treat yourself to some new needles when working French knots – they'll make them that much easier.

126 Is it better to complete each cross stitch individually or work them in twos?

You can use both methods within the same design. Some areas are more suited to working in rows, for example, solid areas of colour, and others to working the stitches individually, for example, colours dotted around to make up a flower.

127 How do I secure my backstitch thread in position?

If there are no other stitches that you can use to anchor the thread in, you will need to hold the end of the thread by placing your thumb at the back of the fabric while making the first stitch. Then catch it under your first few backstitches until it is secure.

128

Use French knots to create berries on holly and seeds on strawberries. French knots on animals can really make them come to life too.

129 How can I stop my backstitch making the holes in the fabric appear larger?

It sounds as though you are pulling the thread too tightly as you work the backstitch. Try and relax a little and don't pull the thread too tightly otherwise you will distort the fabric and the backstitch won't look good at all.

130

When you are pulling the thread through on a French knot, be gentle as you could tighten it too much and lose the knotted effect.

131 A Holbein stitch is also known as double running stitch. A row of running stitch is worked in one direction, missing out alternate squares, and then the empty squares are completed on the return journey with your needle and thread. This technique is often used in Blackwork.

132 **Why do so many cross stitch designs have backstitch added to them?**
Backstitch is a great way to add definition to designs, particularly small designs, where there is limited space for detailed shading. In larger designs, the backstitch is often more subtly used. Backstitch is also great for adding detail to the faces of animals, cartoon characters and people, bringing them magically to life.

133 A French knot is a tiny knotted stitch that is added to embroidery to give texture and depth. They are also perfect for adding detail such as eyes to a stitched design.

134 **Is there a preferred way for left-handers to work backstitch?**
If you are left handed you may find it easier to work the backstitch outlines from left to right and from the top to the bottom of the fabric.

135 **My French knots look rather long and thin, rather than round – what can I do?**
You've probably wound the thread more than twice around the needle to create a longer, Bullion knot.

136 Can I stitch backstitch well enough if holding the fabric in my hand?

You will probably find it much easier with a hoop. This will hold the fabric taut and flat so that you can add the backstitch with neat results.

137 It's tempting to work straight stretches of backstitch as one long stitch to speed up your stitching, rather than working lots of small stitches. If you do this you may find that your tension is not as good and the finished appearance of your stitching may also look untidy. Long stitches don't sit as securely along a line as a shorter backstitch will.

138 How do I keep track of backstitch when there is a lot in a design?

You will find it helpful to have a range of coloured pencils by your side as you stitch. When working on a particular shade of backstitch, use a coloured pencil to shade in the line as you stitch, so that you can see at a glance exactly where you are. Use a different coloured pencil for each of the different shades of backstitch used in the design and you'll feel confident about where you are.

139 Backstitches can run in any direction – left, right, back, forward or diagonal – and are usually worked in a darker shade than the neighbouring cross stitch (or sometimes a contrasting light colour). They can be likened to an outline on a drawing. They can be worked in one or two strands, depending on the amount of definition needed in the design.

140 **How can I stop my Algerian eyes from looking messy?** You need to take care with your tension when working an Algerian eye. Pull the thread tight enough to form an attractive pattern around the centre hole, as if you leave the stitches too loose the 'wheel spokes' won't be clearly defined enough to make the pretty stitch.

141 Wherever possible each backstitch should be the same length as a cross stitch. This will give your stitching a neat and professional finish.

142 When adding long stitch to a design, make sure that the fabric is stretched taut in a frame. This will ensure that your long stitches have a good tension and lay neatly on top of the fabric.

143 **How do I work a backstitch that finishes in the middle of a square?** Often on faces and other areas of detail, a shorter backstitch is needed and the backstitch ends in the middle of the square. If you are using aida fabric you will need to pierce a hole in the centre of the aida block for this small stitch. However, if you are using evenweave you can use the hole that is already available.

144 Assisi work is a type of stitching where the outline is stitched first and then the background is filled in with cross stitch, leaving the area inside the outline 'void' or unstitched.

145 Always try and keep any diagonal backstitches lying parallel to one arm of the cross stitch, so your stitching looks neat.

146 If you stitch French knots too small, try stitching with a thicker thread or use more strands together in the needle and then work the knot as normal for a 'fatter' result.

Charts & kits

147 Each square on the cross stitch chart for a design has a symbol in it and each symbol corresponds to one whole cross stitch.

148 The key that comes with a chart will list the colours that are to be used for each of the symbols, so that you know which colour to thread your needle with as you stitch the design.

149 Many cross stitch designs suggest that you backstitch in black. As this can sometimes look harsh, try using a charcoal grey instead, such as DMC 413.

150 **What are the different elements included in a cross stitch kit?**
In a cross stitch kit you should get everything needed to complete the design. The kit will include the fabric, the threads, the chart and a needle. There should also be instructions as to how to stitch the design and in some kits you get a thread organiser to keep your threads tidy and neatly arranged for use.

151 If more than one skein of thread of a colour is needed for a design, this information should be given alongside the listing of that colour in the key.

152 If you like experimenting with different fabrics and threads, buy charts rather than kits, as then you can choose your own fabric and choose some different threads to use in the design if you prefer.

153 Is it OK for me to photocopy a chart?
Many magazine publishers are happy for their charts to be photocopied for your own personal use. This means that you can keep the original chart in pristine condition and work from your photocopy, making any necessary notes and marking on the chart as you stitch the design. But always check with companies such as DMC, Coats Crafts and Designer Stitches. You should never sell a photocopied chart for financial gain.

154 What can I expect to find in a chart pack?
A chart pack will usually contain the chart plus any embellishments that are used in the design, such as buttons and beads. It may also contain pre-cut lengths of specialist threads, such as variegated threads or pure silks that would be expensive to buy separately.

155 If you are new to cross stitch, go to a specialist needlecraft shop where the assistants will be able to help you. Choose a kit that doesn't use too many colours and that is stitched on 14-count aida. It's best not to choose too large a design for a first project, so that you finish it fairly quickly and get a sense of satisfaction from it.

156 Manufacturers are now required to state fabric measurements in centimetres. This can be confusing when the fabric counts are calculated in holes per inch. To convert inches to centimetres simply multiply by 2.5.

157 **How to I find the centre of the chart?**
Many charts in magazines have their centre clearly marked. However, some other charts may not be as easy to use, so to find the centre, first count the stitches across the design and mark the halfway point. Draw a vertical line in pencil down the design at this point. Next, count the stitches down the design and again mark the halfway point with a pencil. Draw a horizontal line away from this mark, and the point where the two lines cross is the centre of the design.

158 Try and protect a chart from dirt. If you are working a large design over several months, the chart can get rather grubby. You can prevent this from happening by having your chart laminated, so that any spills or marks can be wiped off. Most high street photocopying shops are able to offer this service if you ask.

159 **When I use the threads in a kit I sometimes run out before I've finished - why?**
Make sure that you are only using two strands instead of three, if that is how you are instructed to stitch the design on the chart.

160 **If DMC threads are recommended with a chart, would it matter if I substituted some Madeira threads for some colours?**
It is best to stick with one brand or the other unless you are a very experienced stitcher and can accurately match like DMC to like Madeira threads.

161 **How are symbols chosen on charts?**
The main purpose of the symbols is to make it as clear as possible for the stitcher to read the chart and stitch the design, so fonts are specially created with easy-to-read, clear symbols that make the charts as accessible and uncomplicated-looking as possible.

162 If you have created some of your own charts, why not try selling them at a stall or in a charity shop? With computer programs and colour printers it is quite easy to put together a chart with a pack front – you never know, you might find yourself with a new business to run!

Fabric

163 Aida is the fabric that most stitchers use when they first take up cross stitch. The fibres are woven into bundles, creating blocks of fabric, with evenly placed holes in between. Because the holes are very uniform and easy to see it makes the perfect choice for your first stitching project.

164 Use small, leftover pieces of fabric to stitch small designs such as fridge magnets, keyrings and bookmarks. Store them away through the year and then give them as extra stocking filler-size presents at Christmas.

165 If you're working on a darker-coloured fabric, pre-rinse it before starting to stitch to make sure that the colour doesn't run.

166 When stitching on plastic canvas, always try and choose a design that is quite densely stitched as you will find that plastic canvas works best when there is little or none of the canvas left showing. It doesn't look attractive 'peeking through'.

167 Afghans are traditionally stitched for babies, but also make a wonderful addition to a sofa or chair. Afghan fabric is like aida in that it is woven with an even number of vertical and horizontal threads, making it suitable for counted cross stitch. It is much more loosely woven than aida and has a rather stretchy feel to it, making it perfect for a cot blanket or throw.

168 Perforated paper is a thin card that is punched with a grid of holes. It is available in 14-count and can be stitched in just the same way as you would aida. This is ideal for items such as Christmas tree decorations, children's hanging mobiles and quick bookmarks for gifts.

169 **Can I cut my piece of perforated paper before stitching on it?**

It's a good idea to work out the finished size of the design and cut the paper as you would fabric, so that a margin will be left once the design is complete. Cutting the paper to size makes it easier to handle and you are less likely to damage the paper as you stitch, although extra care must be taken not to tear it when you are stitching.

170 Damask is softer and silkier than regular aida as it is a mix of cotton and rayon. It has an attractive sheen to it, making it ideal to use when stitching for special occasions.

171 **I bought some fabric that seems stiffer than normal. Is it OK to use?**

You can often pick up 'budget' versions of aida and evenweave at market stalls and some stitching shows, but the quality won't be as good as the original fabrics. However, this fabric is fine for stitching small designs such as cards and small pictures, but it is not advised to stitch a large project on such material or one that you are likely to particularly treasure.

172 What can I stitch with waste canvas?
The possibilities for using waste canvas are endless. As long as you can stitch through the fabric and get the needle in and out, you may stitch designs on to clothes, bed linen and many home accessories. It's even possible to stitch on to thicker fabrics such as velvet and denim.

173 When using waste canvas, is it necessary to dampen the threads to remove them?
Some stitchers prefer to dampen the threads, but it isn't always necessary. If you do dampen the canvas, only do so slightly, and then wash the fabric afterwards to remove any sticky residue.

174 What do I do if I find some waste canvas threads difficult to pull out?
This can happen if you have stitched through one of the waste canvas threads with your cotton and stitched the thread down. It's important to ensure that each arm of the cross stitch passes through the centre of the holes on the canvas to so that the threads don't become caught up with one another. Your waste canvas patch will look messy if you can't pull the threads out easily.

175 Waste canvas is a fabric that has been produced to enable cross stitch designs to be stitched directly on to virtually any fabric. It looks rather like a needlepoint canvas, but the warp and weft threads are not interlocked. This enables the canvas to be frayed and the threads pulled apart, to leave the stitching in place on garment.

176 Is it more economical to buy fabric by the metre or in a pack?

It depends on what sort of fabric you want to use and the amount you will need for your design. Once you know exactly what you need you have to decide which is the best way to buy it. Buying a large piece of fabric off a roll is great if you know you are going to use it, so you may want to choose to buy something like white or cream fabric by the metre as you can use if for virtually any project. However, if you know you need an unusual shade of fabric for a one-off design, you will often find you have to buy it pre-packaged as the retailer may not stock it by the metre.

177 What can I use 20-count evenweave fabric for?

20-count fabric is popular for Hardanger work, but you can also use it for cross stitch. Either work over two threads of the fabric using four strands of thread to create a bold design, or work a delicate project using one strand of cotton over one thread of the fabric.

178 Linen is an ideal fabric for creating an authentic-looking sampler or an heirloom piece that you hope will last for years. It is an evenweave fabric that is woven from fibres found in the stem of the flax plant. The threads alternate between thick and thin throughout the weave. The thick part is known as the 'slub' and gives the fabric a wonderful texture that sets off a cross stitch design perfectly. Experiment with this beautiful fabric.

179 I'm stitching on perforated paper and have torn the paper. What can I do?

Stick a small piece of transparent tape to the wrong side of the paper, covering the tear, to join the torn edges carefully back together. Carry on stitching as normal, although you will need to use a sharp needle to pierce through the tape when working on the holes that it covers.

180

Linda fabric is a 100 per cent cotton evenweave fabric made by Zweigart for DMC. It is available in six shades in 27-count. This is an ideal fabric to choose for a first project on evenweave.

181 How many strands of cotton should I use when stitching on perforated paper?

As the holes in the paper are slightly larger that in regular 14-count aida, it is best to use three strands of thread. This will give a good coverage of the paper and prevent light shining through any holes.

182

To stitch successfully on aida band, plan well. You are working in a space just a few centimetres/inches in height and it helps to think carefully about what you can realistically stitch in that size of area. Bear in mind that a design too small will be swamped by the band itself. Choose a design that fits snugly within the borders, with a margin of approximately 4-8 stitches at both the top and bottom, to make the most out of both the design and the decorative aida band itself.

183 Aida or linen band is very versatile and can be used in lots of different ways. Try wrapping it around a special celebration cake, making a quick bookmark, adding interest to towels, personalising a child's gym bag, giving a designer touch to bed linen, or making stunning tie backs for your curtains. You can use a favourite motif again and again, as long as it fits on the band.

184 **Is plastic canvas available in different counts?**
Plastic canvas is available in 7-, 10- and 14-count, so you can use if for bold projects as well as more detailed designs.

185 **Can I stitch any cross stitch design on to a piece of plastic canvas?**
You can't work fractional stitches on to plastic canvas as there is no central hole and it would be very difficult to make one. However, you can stitch any other design as long as it is worked in whole stitches and backstitch.

186 Wherever possible always work a design that contains fractional stitches on to an evenweave fabric. This will enable you to stitch the fractional stitches so much more easily.

187 When stitching on an Afghan fabric, experiment with the number of threads needed to give good coverage before starting on the design for real.

188 **Can I use other types of threads on plastic canvas?** You can stitch with any of the threads you would use on regular fabric and you can also stitch with metallic threads and add embellishments such as beads, buttons and charms.

189 When adding outlines to a design using waste canvas, use a Holbein stitch rather than backstitch as this will produce a much neater outline.

190 Don't cut your piece of waste canvas too close to the stitched design, otherwise you will find it difficult to get a good grip on the canvas threads when you need to pull them out.

191 **What sort of threads should I use when stitching on 10-count plastic canvas?** Try using pearl cotton or tapestry wool on this count of canvas as this has large holes and will need a thick thread to cover it well. You can use plastic canvas to experiment with threads and use anything that gives a good coverage of the canvas. This would be a good way for a beginner or child to start stitching.

192 When stitching on evenweave in a hoop, don't worry which way up your fabric is before you start stitching. As the name suggests, evenweave is evenly woven, so the appearance is the same whichever way up it is.

193 When stitching white areas, such as snow or clouds, on to a dark fabric, use an extra strand of thread in your needle. For example, if working on 28-count evenweave/14-count aida, use three strands instead of two. This will give a much denser coverage of the fabric and make the finished design look better, and ensure that none of the dark material shows through the white.

194 If you find fabric a little stiff, give it a gentle wash before starting to stitch on it. This should soften the fabric and make it much easier to work on.

195 **How many strands of thread do I need to use when stitching on an Afghan fabric?**
This is really a matter of personal choice, depending on how much you want the colours to stand out. Use at least four strands when stitched over two threads on an 18-count Afghan and between four and six strands over two threads on a 14-count Afghan.

196 Binca is a fabric with a low stitch count. It is really useful for teaching children to stitch, as well as adults who may have problems with their eyesight and find finer fabrics quite difficult to use.

197 Aida band is a narrow strip of aida that has been finished off with decorative trimming. It is great for adding a cross stitch design to a towel, just choose a colour to suit your bathroom.

198 Plastic canvas is made from sheets of plastic, punched with a mesh of holes. These holes are used for stitching a design on to the canvas, just as you would on to fabric.

199 When pulling out waste canvas threads, you may find a pair of tweezers helpful to get a strong grip on the threads.

200 Cut your fabric at least 5-8cm (2-3in) larger all round than the size of your finished design. This will give you enough fabric for framing at the end, and also allow you to put your stitching in a scroll frame or hoop. If you want to put a coloured mount around the design in the frame, you might find it beneficial to add a slightly larger margin. It all adds up to a more professional finish.

201 **What colour of plastic canvas should I use?**
Many stitchers prefer to use the clear type of plastic canvas, because, once the design is stitched on to the plastic, the remaining margin of plastic can hardly be seen. However, if you want to choose a colour, try and select a shade which ties in with a colour used in the design you are stitching. You will find plastic canvas in red and blue, green and yellow, in both bold and pastel shades, as well as many other colours.

202 Store your sheets of perforated paper in a cardboard backed envelope to keep it flat and free from creases, which would spoil it for stitching.

203 You will need to bind the edges of your fabric to prevent them from fraying while you stitch. You can do this by machine or hand. Turn the edges under by 5mm and then 5mm again and sew the hem in place. These stitches don't need to be very neat as they won't be seen. If you have a sewing machine, zig zag stitch around the edges of the fabric.

204 Start stitching from the centre of the chart and on the centre of the fabric. To find the centre of the fabric, all you have to do is fold it in half, first vertically and then horizontally. Where the two folds cross is the centre. Some stitchers find it helpful to mark each of these centre lines with a line of tacking stitches, so they can refer to them while they are stitching. Use a pale tacking cotton, as a darker shade can sometimes leave a slight mark when removed.

205 If you find perforated paper difficult to hold as you stitch, stick the paper to the back of an empty picture frame with masking tape that you can carefully peel off without tearing the paper. This will help keep it in position and give you something to hold on to.

206 When you have finished stitching a plastic canvas design, you can finish it off by oversewing all round the edge or attach it to black card. To make a three-dimensional shape, oversew the pieces together to gradually build up a structure. A gift box works very well.

207 To stitch on plastic canvas work out the finished size of your design and cut your canvas 3cm ($1^1/2$in) larger all round. Cover the cut edges with masking tape to prevent your thread from snagging while you stitch. You should find the masking tape easy to remove when you have finished stitching your design on the canvas.

208 Perforated paper can have jagged edges where it has been cut. Carefully trim these edges so that they don't catch on the thread as you stitch.

209 Plastic canvas is great for teaching others to stitch as the canvas can be cut to a shape that is comfortable to hold in the hand and it is also much more rigid than fabric, making the holes easier to see.

210 Stitch a design in the centre of a cut piece of plastic canvas. On 14-count you will probably need three strands instead of the usual two. Start and finish off the thread securely on the back by running it under the back of your stitches. You can stick card on the back of the canvas when you have finished with double-sided sticky tape.

211 Many people end up just stitching on white aida or evenweave. Try stitching on cream aida and linen for a change. Navy and black can also create dramatic backdrops for a design as long as a bright, contrasting coloured thread is dominant.

212 When using plastic canvas, cut your design to shape when you have finished all the stitching. Use general purpose craft scissors rather than embroidery ones and cut carefully around the design, leaving a border of one unstitched bar all around. This will keep your stitches in place. Try to cut in a straight line between two holes and trim off any jagged points afterwards.

Designing

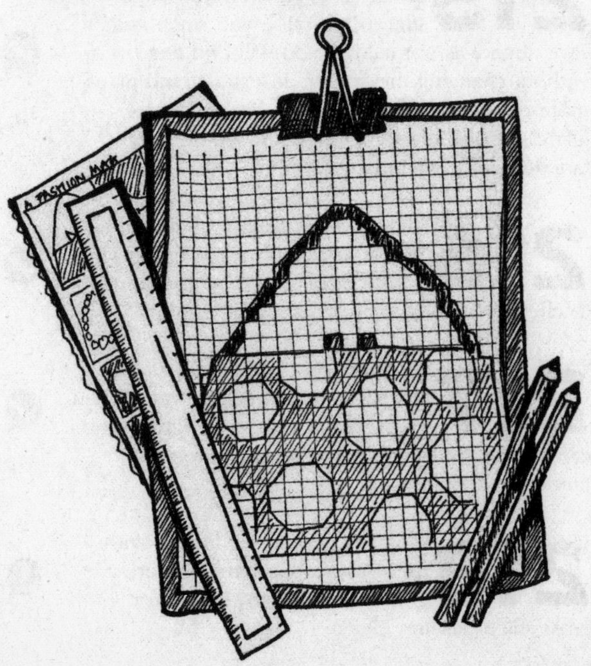

213 Graph paper and coloured pens are the simplest tools you'll need to start designing.

214 Decide on the finished size of your design before you start drawing and also the type of fabric you want it to be stitched on. You can then calculate the chart size using the fabric count. Once you have the finished chart size you will be able to decide how much detail to include in the design.

215 An easy way to add depth to a design is to vary the number of strands of cotton you stitch with. Two strands is normal but you will find that even without changing the colour, an extra strand gives more depth and dimension to a design just as using just one strand makes for much 'thinner', faded-looking stitching.

216 Stitch a small sample of your design, preferably a section that incorporates all the main colours, to check that everything works well together.

217 A scrapbook of designs, pictures and patterns will inspire you. When you're ready to start designing you can lift out the samples that you need for a particular design.

218 Children's colouring books, with their simple line drawings, are a great source of inspiration for cross stitch designs.

219 To give you confidence when you are designing, choose a subject you enjoy, like gardening or animals, and get inspiration from books, magazines, wrapping paper, cards – you will find sources of inspiration all around you.

220 How can I overcome difficulties when I'm trying to design realistic charts on squared graph paper?

You will find it helpful if you forget about the restrictions of the squared grid on the graph paper. First, draw your design idea on to a plain piece of paper and then use tracing graph paper to transfer them, staying as close as possible to your original sketch. This should help ensure that your finished design looks natural rather than 'square'. Remember backstitch always help add realistic detail, as do fractional stitches.

221 Try and really use the fabric you are stitching on, rather than it just being something on which to stitch your design. For example, it's quicker to stitch fluffy white clouds on to a light blue fabric, than stitch an entirely solid blue sky on to plain white material. Navy aida is perfect for a night sky, too.

222 What size designs should I start off with?

Keep it simple for your first attempt. Start off with a small design, for something like a card, measuring no more than 50x50 squares. Once you have completed one design and got the feel for it, you will feel encouraged and inspired to move on to larger projects.

223 **Where can I get inspiration for cross stitch designs?** Anywhere and everywhere. Be aware of current fashions and design trends. Visit home furnishing and DIY stores to see the different styles available, and card shops to see which top styles are selling fast.

224 When designing a sampler, draw the motifs on to one piece of graph paper, then cut them all out and arrange them on a second sheet of graph paper so that you can move them around until they create a balanced design.

225 **Is it better to design using pen and paper or a computer?** Some designers only use pens and paper, or coloured markers and felt tips pens; others use computers, and some use a mixture of both, sketching out their design first before transferring it on to the computer. Computers can save a great deal of time when it comes to designing and can give you information on what the design will look like when stitched. Many companies that sell designing packages are very happy to send you a demonstration disc before you make your final choice regarding which package you are going to buy.

226 Try to avoid using black as a backstitch outline as this can look rather severe. Look at the colours used throughout your design and pick a darker shade of colour that has already been used to give a softer finish to your stitching.

227 How do I sell my designs?

Firstly, ask yourself whether your designs are good enough to be published and check the market to see if yours are that little bit different from what is already out there. If you want to work for a magazine, then choose a magazine whose designs you like and send some samples of your work to the editor. Do the same if you want to work for a specific company, phoning first to see who you need to send your designs to. Alternatively you can decide to set up your own company and make designs in to kits to sell, perhaps through the classified ads in a stitching magazine. With computers and colour printers this is becoming much simpler to do.

228 Can I use knitting patterns of cartoon characters and transfer them to cross stitch?

It is not a good idea to use knitting patterns for cross stitch as an individual stitch is a square, whereas a knitting stitch is a rectangular shape. The pictures that are designed for knitting are charted with this in mind and if you try to cross stitch them the characters will end up looking distorted.

229

Photographs of any designs you create yourself can be assembled in a portfolio – a great advert if you wish to try and sell your designs, and useful for showing off, too!

230

Tracing graph paper is available in a range of different counts, from 11 right up to 22 holes per inch. It's available from most good stitching shops.

231 Is there a limit to how many colours I should use in a design?

It is up to you, but sometimes using a limited amount of colours can produce a more harmonious design as they all tie in with each other. Many designers select just five or six colours of thread and then choose a light, medium and dark shade in each of the colours. This allows them to use more colours in the design, but also helps bring the design together.

232 Is there a particular brand of thread that is best for a designer to use?

Most designers have their own particular favourite brand of thread, usually selecting to use one of the three major manufacturers – DMC, Anchor or Madeira. Once you have chosen the brand you want to use, invest in a shade card for that manufacturer so you can see the entire range of colours available at a glance.

233 How are the colours listed on a shade card?

On a shade card, you will find that all the colours are grouped together in colour rather than in numerical order. For example, first the yellows, followed by the browns, the reds, the pinks etc. If you look more closely you will notice that the shades are also grouped by colour family – for example, all the reddish yellows are together, then all the brownish yellows. Try to pick lighter and darker shades of a colour from the same colour family to use in a design. This will create realistic, graduated effects.

234 When adding blocks of lettering to a design, try using variegated threads to add interest to an otherwise very simple area of the design.

235 Why do the colours often look darker on the fabric than they appear on the skein?

This happens because the second arm of the cross stitch creates a slight shadow across the thread, making it appear slightly darker. Although the effect is very slight, it is something to bear in mind when selecting colours for a design, especially if it is densely stitched.

236 Save all your designs, even the ones you think are unusable. You may come back to them at a later date and see that a few changes here and there could make all the difference.

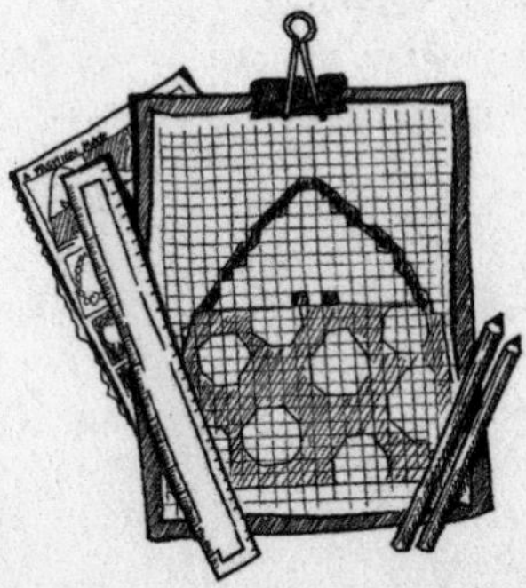

Needles

237 A needle with a blunt end, like a tapestry needle, is best for cross stitch. These are available in a range of different sizes suitable for the different counts of fabric.

238 The size of needle you use for cross stitch depends on what count of fabric you are working on. If you want to stock up on the most common sized needles used for cross stitch, then sizes 24 and 26 are the best to buy.

239 If you keep your needles in a pin cushion, try leaving a length of thread in them. This way, they are easier to pick out from the pins when you next want to use one.

240 Don't be tempted to place needles in the arm of a chair on on a table if you need to leave your stitching for a few moments. It's all to easy to forget about them entirely and someone else might find out, the painful way, where you left them.

241 **My needle is catching on my thread – what's wrong?**
After a while, all needles wear a little, and the tiny imperfections on their surface can cause them to rub against your fabric. When this happens it's definitely time to change your needle. As needles are an inexpensive item of your workbox, it's worth keeping a good supply of needles in stock so that you always have one spare in the size you need.

242 Beading needles are often longer than other needles. This flexible needle is used primarily on bead looms to make jewellery etc, and although you can use them for cross stitch, it is more convenient and safer to use the shorter ones that are now available for beading.

243 A magnetic needle holder is a great way to keep needles safe and secure while you stitch.

244 To thread a needle with stranded cotton, loop the thread end over the end of the needle and pull it tight. Slip the folded end off the needle and, holding it securely between your fingers, insert it through the eye.

245 Why is my cross stitch needle called a tapestry needle?
Tapestry needles are not only used for tapestry, but many different types of counted thread embroidery, including both tapestry and cross stitch. Some manufacturers package needles labelled suitable for cross stitch and these are obviously fine to use as are any packaged as tapestry needles.

246 I have a nickel allergy and find tapestry needles irritate my skin. Any alternatives?
Choose gold-plated needles as these will prevent your allergy from flaring up. In time the gold plating will wear off, so be ready to change your needle when this happens.

247 **I stored my needles in a cupboard and they have rusted – why?**
Perhaps the cupboard is slightly damp. This would cause the needles to rust. Try and store them in a completely dry place so that they remain rust free.

248 Never leave your needle in the fabric in between stitching sessions. If the nickel plating becomes tarnished it will mark the fabric.

249 **I need to add beads to a design – what size needle should I use?**
Use a very fine size 28 tapestry needle to add beads to your stitching, or buy a beading needle.

250 Gold-plated needles are given an extra coat of gold on top of the usual nickel plating. This makes them very smooth to sew with and longer lasting. They are more expensive, but worth the investment.

251 'Gold-eyed' needles are unlike normal gold-plated needles, where the plating rubs off after use, as they are plated only on the eye, so the gold doesn't rub off as the needle passes through the fabric.

252 Use a needle threader – these are widely available at haberdashery departments and stitching shops. Insert the loop of fine wire on the threader through the eye of the needle. Thread the cotton through the wire loop and pull the loop back through the needle, taking the thread with it.

253 When using a fine needle on a delicate fabric, cut a strip of thin paper 5cm (2in) long, narrower than the eye of the needle. Fold the strip in half and place the thread inside. Insert the paper through the eye of the needle, taking the thread with it.

254 **Why am I finding it tricky stitching a design on to fabric using waste canvas?**

This is probably the only occasion when it's a good idea to use a crewel needle to work in cross stitch. Tapestry needles will pass through some fabrics easily, but if it is a thick fabric such as denim, then a crewel needle is called for.

255 **How do I know what size needle I am using?**

When you buy your needles the size will be on the packet. If you have thrown the packet away, the simplest way to gauge the size of your needle is to pass it through the fabric that you are going to be working on. If the needle needs to be pushed through the fabric and distorts the hole, then it is too large. On the other hand, if it falls straight through then you can tell it is too small.

Taking photos & photo-charting

256 Plenty of photocharting companies are available to create a chart for you and can be found on the internet or advertised in magazines. It is helpful to be able to see a sample of one of the company's charts before picking one to send your photo to.

257 If the subject on a photo that you want photocharted is quite small, and you want it bigger, mention your requirements to the photocharting company. They will look at the photo and see if it possible to zoom in on the main subject of the picture, without affecting the clarity of the finished design.

258 Sepia tones make effective photo charts and you will get a very impressive result – but be prepared for some hard work with lots of shades to stitch. It's well worth the effort though.

259 **Do holiday snaps make good subjects for photocharting?** Anything is a good subject for photocharting as long as your main subject is clear and in focus, without too much detail around it. If a place or person is special to you, then it is a good subject.

260 If possible, take pictures of your stitching outside in natural light. This will eliminate the need for the flash on the camera and will give a much more realistic representation of the colours in the design that you are photographing.

261 Why does a photochart I have need 70 shades of thread? It is so expensive!

To achieve detailed results, some pictures require lots of colours in a wide variety of very similar shades. However, most photocharting companies will give you a choice of how detailed you want your finished design to be and, in turn, how many colours of thread you will need. Speak to the company about this before submitting your design so that you don't get too much of a shock when you realise you have to buy loads of new shades of thread to complete the design!

262 Is it possible to have old photographs charted, like antique wedding photos?

Anything can be charted for you to stitch and sepia photos like yours work very well as photo charts. Remember to ask for your precious photograph back once the charting is complete.

263 If you stitch a lot of pictures as gifts, keep a photo album of your stitching, so that you have something to show for all your efforts.

264 Uncluttered pictures work best as subjects for photocharting, so choose your subjects carefully.

265 A photocharting company can 'remove' an item from a photo if you don't want it on the chart. When you send them a photo, highlight the area you want charted with a tracing paper overlay.

266 Can you give me some advice on taking pictures of my stitching?

It's a good idea to take the picture of your design before you have it mounted behind glass. Otherwise the flash may bounce off the glass.

267

It's important that you take a picture of your design with the camera directly above or in front of the stitching. This will ensure that the stitched piece looks as it does in real life and is in perspective. If the picture is taken with the design sloping away from the camera, then the base of the design will be photographed fairly clearly, but the top area of the design may end up looking distorted and out of focus.

268 Is it better to take a picture with a 'normal' camera or a digital one?

There is no difference really – the usual guidelines apply with either. It is just easier to get the images on to your computer and send them to friends and family if you use a digital camera. If you are clever, you can use software on your computer to enhance any areas of your stitching where the colour doesn't seem as bright as it should do in an image.

269 When I take a picture of my stitching, how do I give people an idea of how large or small the project was?

The simplest way to do this is to have someone holding the stitching. Then people will get an idea of the projects size in comparison with the person holding it.

270 I got a photochart back from a company and it seemed very flat – what should I do?

It sounds like they might not have used a great variety of shades. This is a decision/balance you have to make. The more shades, the more detail, the more expensive. Maybe you asked them not to use too many shades and had a budget for the chart. Talk to them and see if they can add a few more shades and ask how much the new price would be.

271 For an unusual photochart, instead of asking for a photochart in sepia tones, why not ask for it to be created in shades of blue, green, pink or red? The result will be a very unique design.

Disasters

272 Print shops will laminate charts for you to stop them from getting worn, creased or tattered.

273 You can avoid eyestrain by stitching in good daylight or use a lamp with a daylight bulb.

274 If your thread collection looks like a birds nest, take some time to sort them out. If the threads are really knotted up, throw them away and start again.

275 If your stitches don't cover the fabric, check that you are using the correct material count and the right number of threads.

276 **I want to stitch a small design from a bigger picture, but it doesn't go over the middle of the whole chart – how do I find the centre?**
Find the centre of your fabric by folding it in half and then half again, as normal. To find the centre of your chosen design or motif, count how many stitches high and how many across it is. Then divide each figure by two. Use these numbers to count in from the design edge and find its centre. So for a design that's ten stitches wide and high, you count five stitches and that's the middle

277 **How do I remove fluffy bits of thread from a design when I have unpicked something?**
Wrap a piece of masking tape around your fingers with the sticky side out and gently dab the affected area. The bits of fluff should stick to the tape.

278 To work out how long a project will take to stitch, time yourself stitching for a minute. Count up the number of stitches you have done and multiple this by 60 to get the approximate number you would complete in an hour. Next, multiply the width and height of the design in stitches to get the stitch count and divide this number by the stitches you can complete in an hour. This will give you an approximate stitching time. Remember to add extra time for the backstitch.

279 **How do I stop my stitches looking messy and uneven?** Try 'railroading' – this is where, on the second arm of the cross stitch, you pass the needle in between the two threads, before taking it through the fabric. The result is beautiful, neat, very impressive stitching.

280 Tidy stitching saves money and time. Finish off threads as you go along – you won't have wasteful, long straggly ends to unpick and cut off later.

281 Say no to knots. Knots at the back of your work could make it 'lumpy'. Start and finish off by threading cotton under the back of a few stitches.

282 **How do I remove a needle rust mark from fabric?** Cover the stain in salt and then squeeze lemon juice over the salt. Leave it overnight and then rinse the salt out thoroughly before washing the fabric.

283 If your stitches look uneven make sure you are working the first half of your cross stitch in the same direction. This gives a professional finish.

284 If your stitches look thin and straggly, you may be using the wrong number of strands. Check on your chart to see how many strands you need for the fabric you are working on.

285 **What can I do as I find the symbols on many charts are too small?**
Take your chart along to a local photocopying shop. They will be able to enlarge the chart so that you can see the symbols easily. As long as the chart is for your own use you shouldn't have any problems with copyright.

286 If your threads are twisted, take a moment or two to let your needle hang down from your stitching and the threads will untwist themselves. If you do this every now and then you should avoid twists and knots in the thread.

287 **How do I stop myself from losing my scissors down the back of the sofa?**
Make yourself a scissor keeper and you'll never lose them again. Stitch a small design and make it into a pincushion. Fill it with wadding and tuck a length of cord into the seam as you finish off the edges. Attach scissors to the other end of the cord and tie securely in position.

288 If your needle collection is all jumbled up, gather together pieces of different count materials and see which needles pass easily through the different fabrics. Size 24 needles should pass through a 14-count fabric, and size 26 needles should slide through 28-count fabric. Once you've sorted your needles, keep them in pieces of felt, labelled with the appropriate size.

289 Talcum powder will absorb greasy marks from fabric. Gently wash the stitching after using it.

290 **I've got lots of different-sized fabrics – how can I tell what's what?**

Use a ruler and line the nought up against a hole on the fabric. Now, count away from that hole to the 1in mark on the ruler. You will now know whether the fabric has 11, 14, 16 or 18 holes per inch. Once you've found out the 'HPI' (or 'count') of the fabric, write it on a small label and to stick in the corner of the fabric, so you can tell instantly what count or HPI the fabric is when you need it. For evenweave fabric, count each hole to the inch mark, then divide by two to find out the HPI.

Teaching others

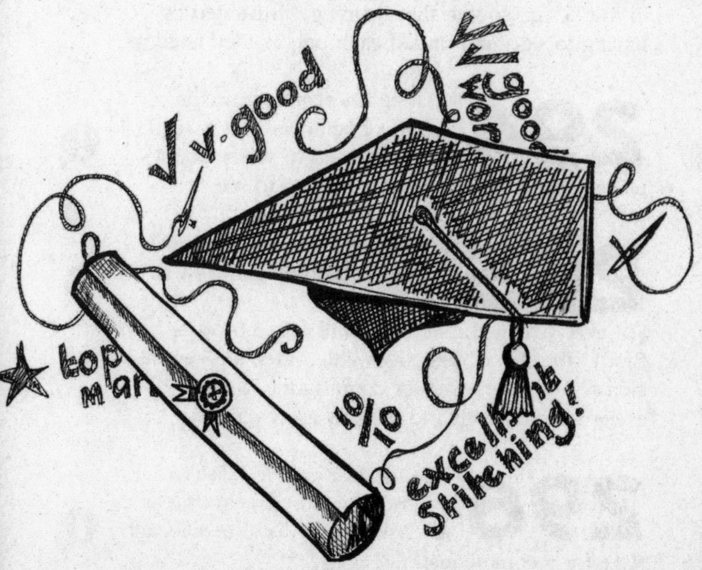

291 If children stitch for a short while to start with, they won't get bored, so give them small designs to stitch.

292 **Is there a thread that is best for children to use?**
A non-divisible thread makes teaching children to cross stitch much easier. Choose a thread such as Soft Cotton from DMC. It's available in a wide range of colours and as there are no strands to divide, a length can be quickly cut and threaded ready for stitching.

293 Threading needles can be boring and difficult, especially for children. When teaching them to stitch, thread several needles with the colours used in the design so that they won't get frustrated by having to stop and thread each one as they need it.

294 Stitching on plastic canvas is good for beginners as it is rigid, you don't need to worry about using a hoop and the holes are easy to see.

295 **What sort of fabric should I buy for teaching children to cross stitch?**
For very young children start off with a 6-count Binca fabric, or if they are a little older, an 8-count aida will be fine. A lower count fabric is much easier to work with and designs grow quickly.

296 Some companies specialise in designs for children as young as four. Ask at your local needlecraft store for recommendations.

297 **Are there any simple designs available for adults to stitch?** For simple designs for an adult, choose any design that is small, uses only a few colours and is free from fractional stitches. Even if the design is recommended to be stitched on a 14-count fabric, you can change it to a fabric with a lower count so that the holes are easy to see and the design grows quickly.

298 Start off teaching the basic rules to beginners, such as always making the top arm of the cross stitch in the same direction, and then bad habits won't need to be corrected later.

299 It helps if you keep organised when teaching, even with the simplest of projects. For beginners, make a thread organiser card by punching holes down a piece of cardboard, add the threads and label accordingly with the symbol and thread number.

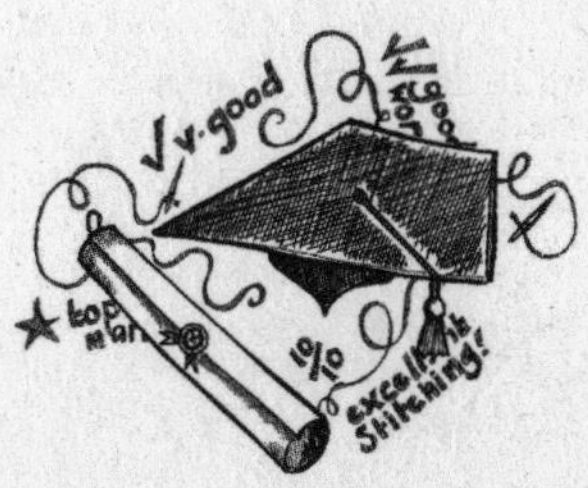

Threads

300 Tweeding is another word for blending. It refers to the use of two different-coloured threads being used in the needle at once to create a 'tweeded' effect. This could be, for example, brown and tan, to show the fur on an animal, or blue and grey used together for the water in a lake. Tweeding is easy to do – once you have combined the required number of strands of the different colours, you thread your needle and work your cross stitches as normal.

301 'Floss' is simply the American term for stranded cotton. You will come across this term in some kits.

302 Always select the thread colours you want to use for a design in good daylight so that you can see exactly what they look like.

303 When using metallic threads, use a larger needle than you normally would. The hole in the fabric is made bigger by the needle and the thread will then pass through more easily.

304 Variegated thread is an embroidery thread where the colour changes along the length of the thread to create a unique pattern when stitched. Use this type of thread for areas where random shades of the same colour are needed, such as on leaves and for skies. Alternatively, use them for stitching borders and single colour designs to create stunning effects.

305 What sort of variegated threads work well for stitching landscape areas?

Choose a thread with a gradual colour change, so that the effect is subtle. Threads with shorter colour changes work best in borders and small projects.

306 What type of fibres are used for variegated threads?

There are four main fibres used for these specialist threads and these are cotton, wool, silk and viscose rayon. The first three are natural whereas viscose rayon is a man-made cellulose fibre.

307 Stranded cotton is a soft, durable thread made from pure cotton. During the manufacturing process it is treated with caustic soda. This gives it a lovely sheen, which makes it good to look at and also smooth to stitch with.

308 The three main manufacturers of stranded cotton are DMC, Anchor and Madeira, all of which produce excellent cotton for cross stitch. You can be sure that the stranded cotton from these manufacturers is colourfast (even when machine washed) so it is perfect for all types of cross stitch.

309 Shade cards are produced by the manufacturer of that particular brand of thread and contain a sample of each of the colours available, with the number of the colour printed next to the sampler. If you are a keen cross stitcher, or a budding designer, then a shade card is a good investment.

310 Blending filament is a very fine sliver of metallic thread. As its name suggests, it is literally a filament that is blended with other threads or stranded cotton. If you have a design that just needs a subtle sparkle or slightly reflective quality, then try using blending filament.

311 Never throw away small lengths of thread. Keep them on an organiser, labelled with the colour, and use when you only need a small amount of thread, for items such as cards, keyrings, magnets etc.

312 Don't store your threads inside a plastic bag where they will gather dust. Invest in a good storage system so that they are kept clean and tidy.

313 Soft cotton threads are where the cotton has not been mercerised (as with stranded cotton). Soft cottons are thick matt cotton threads and are usually used for cross stitch on a low count fabric such as Binca.

314 **I bought some cheap threads and the colours have run – what can I do with them?**
Don't panic! Just keep rinsing the stitching in cold water until the water runs completely clear and no more colour comes out. It's worth remembering that DMC, Anchor and Madeira thread are all guaranteed not to run, so save cheaper, budget threads for quick-stitch projects that don't need washing after you have stitched them.

315 Always wash your hands before handling stranded cotton, as any oils that may be on your hands can rub off on to the cotton and spoil its sheen.

316 **When I stitched with variegated thread I was disappointed with the results - why?**
With variegated threads, try completing each cross stitch before moving on to the next one. This way you will find that the gradual colour changes are shown off to their best. If you work a row of half cross stitch and complete the cross on the way back across the fabric, you may end up with a rather mixed up colour, rather than a clear, gradual change from one shade to another. Just experiment!

317 **Can I mix different brands of thread within a design?**
If you are working on a simple design that uses very definitely different colours, for example, red, yellow, green and blue to stitch something like a beach ball, then you can mix manufacturers as it is the colour that is important rather than the shade. However, when working on a design with detailed shading, it is vital that you use just one manufacturer throughout the design. To end up with exactly the same results as those in the original picture, you must also use the manufacturer whose threads were used to stitch the worked model, otherwise your finished result may be slightly different.

318 Always pull the thread away from the skein in the way it has been wound. The skein will stay in shape and the thread won't tangle up.

319 **How long should I cut thread?** However large the area of a design you are going to stitch, limit yourself to a length of thread no longer than 45cm (18in) – any longer and it may wear and tangle.

320 Always use a new needle when stitching with metallics. It will only cost you a few pence, but will reduce wear and tear on the threads and keep them smooth as you work.

321 If you are using a new type of thread, and are unsure of the number of strands needed, stitch a sample on the fabric to ensure coverage looks ok.

322 **Why do I get in a tangle when I try and pull two strands from a length of cotton?** It sounds to me as if you are pulling both strands away from the cut length at once and this will certainly create a tangle. Instead, pull each strand out individually. Although the thread will bunch up as you do this, you should find that it should free itself once you have pulled out the strand.

323 **How can I keep my threads tidy as I stitch?** The best way to avoid your threads resembling a bird's nest is to select the threads you need for the project you are going to be working on. Once you have assembled them, cut them into lengths, and thread them on to an organiser. Finally, label the organiser with the symbols for each of the threads used in the design.

324 **Can I wash my stitching if I have used metallic threads?** The majority of metallic threads used for cross stitch can be handwashed, but remember to check the symbols on the packet beforehand just in case, as you will find the information you need there. If you are careful you can wash your stitching in water up to the relevant temperature. Do not rub your stitching, but, instead, place your stitching in a pillowcase to protect it from the abrasive action of washing.

325 Be kind to your thread. When stitching, move the needle along the thread from time to time to prevent the thread becoming worn in one place, where it is pulled through the eye.

326 If you get a nasty knot in your length of thread it could just be a very tight 'twist'. Unthread your needle and insert the blunt end into one loop of the 'knot'. Pull gently and it should come free if you are gentle with it.

327 The best thread for cross stitch, or the most commonly used, is stranded embroidery thread. It is made up of six strands which can be easily divided so that you can use the required number of strands for the design you are stitching.

328 Flower thread is made from fine cotton yarn and gives a very subtle effect when used in cross stitch. It cannot be divided into strands, but is cut and used straight from the skin.

329 Try blending a strand of metallic thread with a strand of cotton to work some of the cross stitch on a design. Or substitute red or green metallics for an area stitched in red or green stranded cotton – for example, the berries on a strawberry sampler or a Christmas tree.

330 If you like using metallic threads you will find plenty of designs of Oriental or Indian influence that have twinkling strands of gold or silver in them.

331 **Are variegated threads washable?**
Many of the hand-dyed and variegated threads can be washed by hand, but, because there is such a wide range of manufacturers, it is always advisable to check first to see if the thread you are using is washable. A few companies do not recommend even hand washing because of the dyeing process that has been used, so always check labels or ask before buying them to avoid problems later.

332 To thread metallic thread, when working with a single strand you will find it helpful to cut a small piece of paper and then fold it in half with the end of the thread enclosed in the fold. Now pass the folded strip of paper through the eye of the needle, and in doing so, the thread will also pass through.

333 Don't just use metallic threads for Christmas stitching. Add stars to a sky or substitute it for yellow in a design for an extra special gleam.

334 Do not use long lengths of metallic thread when stitching. It can get worn quite quickly and will either break or even distress the fabric/cotton it is being pulled through.

335 When threading metallic thread, if you are working with an even number of strands, cut a single length of thread, and fold it in half. Feed the looped end through the eye of the needle and then pass over the point to secure the thread in place. This method is also used with blending filament and it will keep the thread firmly attached to the needle and prevent it slipping.

Washing your work

336 Fabrics and threads will mostly have washing instructions on labels, just like clothes. Always check these first before washing anything.

337 To dry your stitching, do not wring the fabric out. Simply roll it up in a clean, dry towel to absorb most of the water. The fabric should be damp, but not dripping.

338 Ironing your stitching after completing a design makes it much more professional-looking.

339 **Can I leave my stitching on a frame in between stitching sessions?**
If you are using a stand with a scroll bar frame you can leave your work in this, but it is advisable to cover it up with a clean piece of cloth, such as a pillowcase, to prevent dust, dirt or spills spoiling your stitching, which can happen all too easily.

340 To iron fabric, place it, stitching side down, on to a clean dry towel. A fluffy towel is best as this absorbs the stitches as you iron, rather than flattens them. Press, with the iron on a low setting until the fabric is dry.

341 **How can I remove a stubborn stain that hasn't come off during washing?**
For difficult-to-remove stains try using a specialist stain remover such as one from the Stain Devils range. Ask your friends what has worked for them.

342 How do I care for an antique sampler?

To clean a dull and dirty sampler, remove it carefully from the frame and clean the glazing using mild soapy warm water. Take great care handling the glass to ensure it doesn't crack. On no account use water to clean the sampler itself as the delicate threads and fabrics used many years ago were dyed without colour-run protection and therefore the slightest bit of water would be a disaster! Instead, clean your sampler using a low power suction cleaner with a fine nozzle. This will reduce some of the loose dust and, even though some dust will not be able to removed, this process should make a surprising difference to the final appearance of the stitching.

343 Try to keep your work clean and tidy while you stitch so that you minimise the need for washing, or, if it does need washing, it's just a quick soak.

344 Can I wash my stitching in a washing machine?

The main thread manufacturers (DMC, Anchor and Madeira) all state that their products can be cleaned in a washing machine on a hot cycle, as long as the stitched piece isn't embellished with any beads or specialist threads, so, if you have a difficult stain you may want to try popping it in the washing machine. Make sure that all the ends of the threads are securely fastened off and place the stitching inside a pillowcase, tying it to secure the end. This will prevent the stitching coming into contact with the rough edges of the washing machine drum.

345 Washing your stitching will make it look brighter and more colourful.

346 A tidy, child- and pet-free work station will help you keep your stitching clean and dirt free.

347 **Does any stitching fabric stand up to washing?**
As with many things, if you buy the best quality product then the answer to this is yes. Good quality fabrics by the main manufacturers are fine to wash both by hand and machine. If you have bought budget fabric, on the other hand, it is probably as well to test a small sample first before stitching a design on it, and then finding it shrinks in the wash.

348 To remove any pet hairs from your stitching, use a pair of tweezers and carefully (and patiently!) remove them one by one.

349 Wash your stitching in lukewarm water mixed with mild soapflakes or detergent. Don't rub the stitching, but let it soak for several minutes. Then, swish it around gently. Rinse thoroughly until the water runs clear, and finally give the last rinse using cold water.

350 If your stitching needs washing, do this before attaching any charms or buttons.

351 Remember to check the colourfastness of beads before washing your stitched piece.

352 **How do I remove a grubby ring mark around my design?** Wash the whole stitching in warm water using a mild detergent. You may have to pay extra attention to the ring mark. Rinse thoroughly, and then roll in a clean dry towel to absorb the excess water.

Stitching websites

353 The internet is a fabulous source of cross stitching information, advice and contacts. If you have a computer, start surfing and a whole world of knowledge will open to you.

354 Cafés and libraries have computers where you can access the internet if you don't have your own computer. At cafés you normally buy a ticket that allows you a certain amount of time on the internet, There will be simple instructions to guide you how to use the computer and get onto the worldwide web. Libraries sometimes offer free access – ask at the information desk

355 **Is it safe to order stitching supplies over the internet?** Yes, as long as you use a secure site (usually denoted by a padlock in the corner of the screen), then your details should be safe. If in doubt, you can browse the site, then phone through your order.

356 To surf the net for cross stitch websites, type in the individual website address, or, alternatively, if you want to just take a look at what's available, go to a search engine such as 'yahoo' or 'google' and type in 'cross stitch'. You will find that many many 'hits' will come up on the screen and then you can browse through them in your own time.

357 You can contact stitchers across the world by using the internet – go on, make some new friends!

358 What sort of websites are available for the cross stitcher?

There are literally thousands of websites concerning stitching. You can find companies selling kits, charts and general materials as well as sites that teach you to stitch or offer you free charts.

359 'Bookmarks' will help you return to a favourite stitching website really quickly.

360 A good site for finding more details about cross stitch is www.cross-stitching.com. You'll find lots of interesting information. Other great sites include www.dmc.com, www.coats-crafts.co.uk and www.yarntree.com.

361 I'm trying to find a specific chart – is there a particular site that is good to try?

Try www.hoffmandis.com as this site lists literally thousands of charts by both designers, themes or your chosen keyword. It's easy to use and gives you pictures of the chart which is very helpful when looking for a particular design.

362 To 'meet' other stitchers online, go to the chat forum on a cross stitch website. Try www.cross-stitching.com and www.aion-needlecrafts.co.uk as a starting point. You can visit the chat rooms and read what visitors are saying before deciding to join yourself. You'll be 'chatting' away with likeminded stitchers before you know it!

Links to free charts and downloads...

363

www.alitadesigns.com/cross-stitch/patterns
Mix of cute and wildlife designs

364

www.americanwhimsy.com/free_cross_stitch.html
Lots of free Celtic designs

365

www.artecy.cjb.net
Can join as a member to receive more designs via email. Two free charts, one quite big.

366

homepage.eircom.net/~andrewsown
Atlantic Stitches – Free Celtic design

367

www.concentric.net/~Nyssa
At River's End – Three small goodie bag designs

Links to free charts and downloads...

368

www.bevscountrycottage.com/x-stitch
Sandy and Bev – Lots of basic charts for beginners

369

www.BirdCrossStitch.com
Lots for the bird enthusiast

370

www.blackworkarchives.com/index.html
Lots of traditional blackwork designs

371

www.brookesbookspublishing.com
Three free charts to download

372

www.charitystitch.co.uk
Free small charts to stitch for charity

Links to free charts and downloads...

373

www.chatelaine.net
Free charts from Germany

374

www.clwydneedlecrafts.force9.co.uk
Three free designs to choose from

375

www.coatscrafts.co.uk
You can create your own cross stitch with a click of a button

376

www.couchmancreations.com.au/freeby.html
Free chart from American Karen Couchman

377

www.countryandcolonial.com
Free chart

378

www.countrystitch.com/freebie.htm
Free chart

Links to free charts and downloads...

379

www.crafts-unlimited.co.uk

Free chart

380

www.cross-stitchandmore.com/chart.htm

Lots of free charts from American designers – Lizzie Kate, Just Nan and more

381

www.crosstitch.com/pdes98.shtm

Lots of categories of free charts

382

www.thecrossstitchguild.com

Free chart plus access to archive when you become a member

383

www.thecrossstitchermagazine.com/freeprojects

Free projects from the American magazine

Links to free charts and downloads...

384

www.crossedwing.com/free/free_charts.html
Free charts of birds

385

www.debbiecripps.co.uk/FreeChart.htm
Free chart

386

www.dididunphy.com
Charts inspired by modern art

387

www.djsdreams.com/freebies.htm
PDF charts to download

388

www.dmc.com/majic/pageServer/0301000000/en_GB/Home.html
Free chart of the week to print

Links to free charts and downloads...

389

www.dmc-usa.com

Free project of the month but will need to download free PC stitch software

390

DragonDreams.accra.ca/samples.html

Free charts of dragons etc

391

www.dunmanidesigns.co.uk

Free charts including blackwork and Assisi designs

392

es.geocities.com/marbhabans/inindex.htm

Spanish Designers site with a free chart

393

www.filanthrope.com/shop/free.asp

Free charts of Chinese designs

394

www.flowerthread.com

Free chart to use with flower thread

Links to free charts and downloads...

395

www.freepatternsonline.com/xspatterns2.htm
Lots of charts to download including blank graphs to design your own

396

www.galacticgallery.net/moreover.html
Free charts

397

www.geocities.com/Wellesley/1912
Two free sampler designs

398

www.gittas.com
Free chart

399

www.haberdasherydesigns.com
Two free charts

400

www.theheartscontent.com
Free chart

Links to free charts and downloads...

401

www.homecrafterssupplycenter.com/freebies.html
Free charts

402

home4.highway.ne.jp/piko/free/chart.html
Four free charts

403

homepage.powerup.com.au/~sheal/freebies.htm
Access lots of charts

404

homespunelegance.net/free_graph.html
Free chart

405

www.hooahdesigns.com/freebie%20archives%20page.htm
Free charts including Assisi and hardanger

406

www.icons.net/~lisajoe
Free design every months

Links to free charts and downloads...

407

www.jaenne.com/Freebie.htm
Free chart

408

www.janbrett.com/cross_stitch/cross_stitch_main_page.htm
Choose from a variety of illustrative designs

409

www.janlynn.com
Lots to choose from Janlynn's designers, including a special chart from the designer of the month

410

www.jeanettecrews.com
Free project every month

411

www.jeanfarish.com/cross_stitch/comp_charts/main_page.htm
Lots to choose from, including Christmas designs

Links to free charts and downloads...

412

www.kittyandme.com/designs.shtml
Free designs from Pamela Kellogg including cats in hats

413

www.koolerdesign.com/freechart.asp
Free charts from one of the Kooler Design Studio designers

414

www.kreinik.com/HTML/freebies/kreinik_freebies.html
Lots of free charts including angels, Christmas and Halloween incorporating Kreinik's glow in the dark thread. Also free plastic canvas, needlepoint and scrapbooking projects

415

www.lenarose.com/freecharts.html
Three free charts

Links to free charts and downloads...

416

www.listen-up.org/htm2/cross.htm
Cross stitch symbols for the deaf

417

www.lizziekate.com/free.html
Free small designs from Lizzie Kate

418

members.madasafish.com/~jillcn
Free blackwork chart

419

www.mariarte.net/index.htm
Become a member to access 14,000 free charts

420

www.maurer-stroh.com/ems.htm
Free designs from US designer Ellen Maurer-Stroh

421

members.aol.com/maluholder
Download two tablecloth charts

Links to free charts and downloads...

422
www.mirabilia.com/crossIndex.html
Downloadable cherubs

423
www.moseynme.com
Hand-drawn downloadable charts

424
www.nostalgianeedlework.com/html/free_designs.html
Download special 'reader' to download free charts

425
www.oldewillowstitchery.com/pages/free.html
Free charts designed on Olde Willow threads

426
www.pkdesigns.com/stitch/celtic.htm
Free celtic knot design

427
www.purpleheart.co.uk/free.php
Three free charts

Links to free charts and downloads...

428

www.ri-va.com/index2.htm
Free Italian designs

429

www.solaria-gallery.com/gobelins/index.html
Free Bulgarian charts

430

solo4.abac.com/lubakmetyk
Lots of free charts of Ukrainian patterns, in colour

431

www.somethingincom.com/free_designs.htm
Clear free charts from America

432

www.stitchalley.com
160 free charts

433

www.stitchingsupplies.com/page13free.htm
Three free charts

Links to free charts and downloads...

434

www.stonedog.co.uk/html/free_charts.html
Free floral charts

435

www.tiag.com
Free chart of a Christmas angel every year plus access to archive from 1986, from Lavender and Lace

436

www.tompudding.co.uk
Everything from Christmas to florals

437

www.treasuredtapestries.com
Lots of free charts from angels to borders

438

www.tristanbrooks.com/PineapplePleasures/Pineapple.htm
Free chart from Tristan Brooks

Links to free charts and downloads...

439

www.twdesignworks.com/Free/index.html
Free charts from Teresa Wentzler, including whitework

440

www.victoriasampler.com
Access free charts when you sign up for the newsletter

441

www.vsccs.com/charts/FreeCharts.html
Free chart added each month. Series for 2004 fantasy bears

442

www.waxingmoondesigns.com/free.html
Lots of free folk art designs

443

www.wildthreads.com/free.html
Free chart

Links to free charts and downloads...

444

www.yarntree.com/007begin.htm
Free chart for beginners

445

www.zianet.com/mikemosier
Free Native American chart

446

www.zweigart.com/frameset_thingstodo.htm
Free tablecloth chart

Finishing & framing

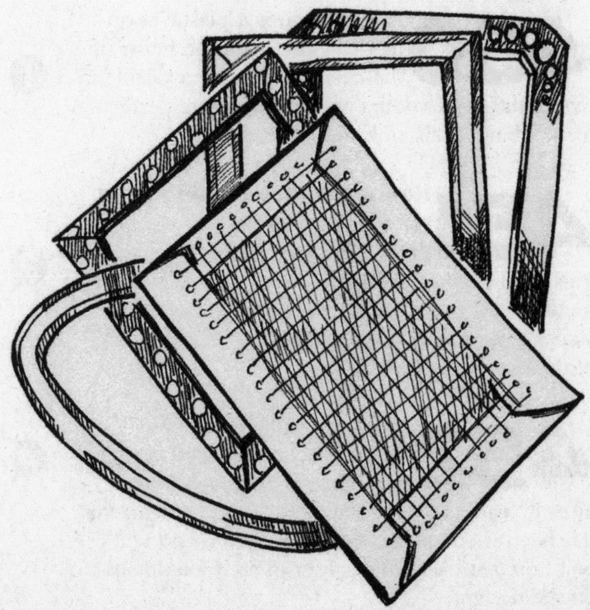

447 Plain wood suits many designs. Choose this if you have trouble in deciding on a colour for the frame or mount for your stitching.

448 Plastic products often come with a sticky price tag or label. Use white spirit to clean up any adhesive residue before mounting your design.

449 Conservation framing uses acid-free mount board. This is ideal to use when mounting heirloom designs, as no acid is going to seep from the board into the fabric and spoil the stitches.

450 A flexi-hoop is a plastic hoop that can also form the frame of the design. They are available in lots of different colours and sizes and are perfect for stitching small, quick-to-finish designs.

451 **How much time should I allow for a design to be professionally framed?**
This usually takes about two weeks, so remember to allow this extra time, especially if you are stitching for a special occasion such as a wedding, birthday or anniversary.

452 When choosing a coloured mount for your stitched design, try and pick out a colour that already features in the stitching. Select a colour that has been used just a little in the design and you will find that using this colour in the frame helps to lift the design.

453 Be adventurous with your choice of mount. If you want to frame the design using an unusually shaped mount, ask your framer if this is possible. It can make all the difference to the final appearance of your stitching.

454 **What sort of frame works best for cross stitch?**
It all depends on the look you want to achieve: do you want to give your stitching an antique look, or an up-to-the-minute style? You will find that plain, natural wood looks good in any setting, while gold or gild gives a special finish to samplers. Framing shops will be happy for you to see the range available and to try out their sample corners against your piece of stitching.

455 **I've stitched a design that is too small for the frame I want to use. What can I do?**
Try using a wide mount, or even a double mount to fill the space between the frame and the fabric. Choose the colours of the mountboard carefully, so that it doesn't detract from the cross stitch.

456 Frames can be found in charity shops and are a good, cheap option. Just take out the old print and mount as you normally would.

457 If you are giving a framed design as a gift, make sure you sign and date the back of the frame for posterity and add a message to the recipient – it will be read by future generations.

458 Always check over your work thoroughly for any omissions or mistakes and make sure it is completely clean before having it framed. It will be too late once the frame is securely in place.

459 **What sort of glass should I use to frame my cross stitch designs?**
If you go to a framer they should be able to advise you on what type of glass to use. You may want to see an example of non-reflective glass as this enables people to see your stitching from all angles, without the light bouncing off it.

460 It's always a good idea to think ahead a little when buying a cross stitch design. Will the size of the design make it expensive to frame, or is it an unusual shape and could this add to the cost?

461 If you are stitching on a budget, visit high street stores where they sell cheap prints in frames. You will often find some interesting frames to use.

462 Coasters, trinket pots, powder compacts and brooches perfectly frame small designs and make great presents to give to friends and family.

463 When mounting designs behind glass that incorporate beads or charms, remember to add extra depth to the frame by using a double, or even triple mount, so that the embellishments don't come into contact with the glass.

464 When stitching a design for a coaster, compare the measurements of the finished design and the size of your coaster before stitching. You may be able to make a design fit better by stitching it on different count fabric.

465 **How do I protect a picture from moisture when hanging it in the bathroom?**

You either need to not put glass in front of your work, so that it can breathe, or make sure that the back of the frame is very well sealed up. Use plastic tape, or even plastic bathroom sealant (the type that comes in tubes) to seal the gaps in the back of the frame. However, even with these precautions you cannot guarantee that your design won't become damaged over time, so it's best to avoid hanging precious pictures in the bathroom and instead use it to display quick-to-stitch designs.

466 To avoid disappointment when mounting a design, it's always best to allow about 3in of spare fabric on each side of your design. So, if the finished size of cross stitch is going to be 8x10in, cut a piece of fabric measuring 14x16in.

Hoops & frames

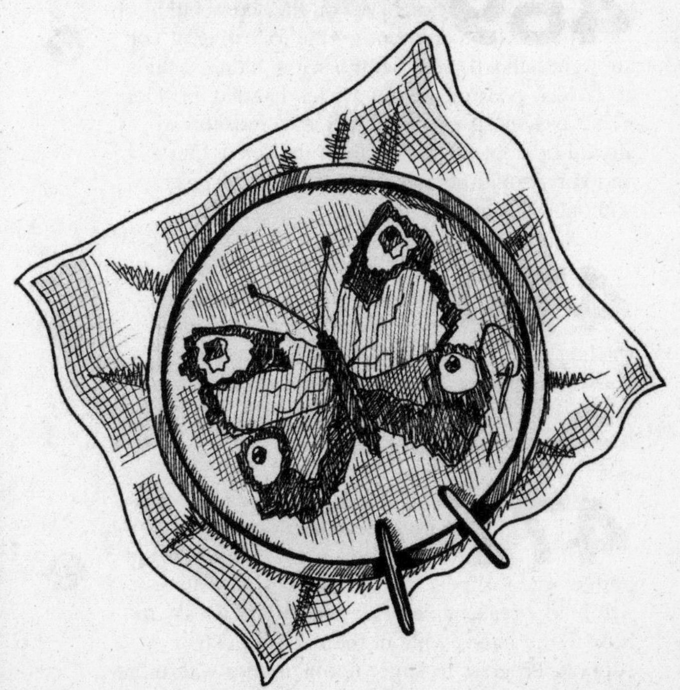

467 Maintaining a uniform tension on the fabric you're stitching on helps make your stitching neater, so always try and use a hoop.

468 Many hoops and frames are available such as flexi-hoops, plastic hoops, clip frames, wooden frames, lap frames and floor-standing frames. Choose what suits you best.

469 To stop your thread from getting caught up on the screw fitting of a hoop, try the following: if you are right-handed, position the screw fitting at the 10 o'clock position; If you are left-handed, position it at 2 o'clock. If you do it this way your thread should be kept well away from the screw fitting and you should be able to stitch smoothly and without interruptions.

470 Spring tension hoops were originally used for machine embroidery, but many cross stitchers now use them. They provide a very constant and even tension, as they are sprung, rather than tightened with a screw. This type of hoop tends to be more expensive.

471 **What is the best sort of hoop to buy for a beginner?**
A 15cm (6in) wooden hoop is the perfect size for most stitchers to start off with as it will hold a reasonable-sized design and is easy to hold in the hands without the need for extra support. Progress to larger hoops/frames with more advanced, larger projects.

472 When should I use a lap frame?

Stitchers who enjoy sitting at a table or who like to stitch with a frame balanced on a lap will prefer this type of frame. Lap frames are quite versatile in that they can be packed flat for storage, or to take away with you on holiday, and they are ideal for those larger projects that are too big for hoops. They don't take up as much room as a floor stand, so if you don't have a great deal of space in the room in which you tend to stitch to leave a floor frame out, this is ideal for you because you can hide it away easily.

473

Using a hoop helps you keep your tension and also evens out small creases that you may have in the fabric. The needles passes through the fabric more easily and the finished stitching is less bulky as the threads lie flat on the fabric. If it doesn't remove the creases in some fabric these will go when you have washed your completed stitching and then ironed it afterwards.

474 When should I use a floor frame?

A floor frame is great for using when stitching large designs. You place your stitching in a hoop or frame as required then attach it to a floor frame. This supports your stitching in a fixed position, leaving both hands free for stitching. The frame also enables you to manoeuvre your work to a comfortable position. This is great to have if you have a good, set area/work station for your stitching, with your own comfy chair that no one else is likely to sit on.

475 **Do I need a floor frame as well as a hoop?**
If you tend to stitch small designs, or stitch on the move, then you won't find a floor frame necessary. However if you like stitching large designs, then you will find this piece of equipment very useful.

476 Always use a hoop that is large enough for the design you are stitching to fit inside. Otherwise you will have to move the hoop around and this could cause your stitches to become squashed and look uneven.

477 Hoops and frames come in many sizes from 10cm (4in) through to 30cm (12in), so there is something available to fit a wide range of projects. If you can't afford bigger frames, make sure you buy designs that will fit in the smaller frame/hoop you have until you can afford a larger frame and then stitch larger projects. With a larger frame on a stand you can clip lights and magnifiers to the edge of the frame, too.

478 If your hoop is distorting the fabric, take a little extra care as you put the fabric in the hoop. Place the top hoop over the bottom hoop and fabric so that it is quite loose and gradually tighten the wing nut until the fabric is taut. The area of fabric in the hoop should have all the threads lying at right angles to each other so that each cross stitch looks 'square' on the fabric.

479 **Which is best - a hoop or a frame?**
It really depends on the size of the design you are stitching. Many stitchers prefer to use hoops for small to medium-sized designs and have a frame for large projects that are going to take several months to complete.

480 Binding the rings of your hoop with a length of cotton ribbon prevents the fabric from becoming marked or snagged by any imperfections in the wooden hoop.

Special occasions

481 **Can you give me some tips for stitching wedding stationery?** If you are going to be stitching a large quantity of the same design you need to keep it simple. Choose a small design that uses only a handful of colours and try to steer clear of fractional stitches, too much backstitch or anything else that is going to take extra time. Time yourself stitching one design and then work out how many hours will be needed to complete the entire set of stationery so that you can work out a timetable for completing the stitching well before the deadline.

482 **How can I keep the costs low when stitching for charity?** If you have a friendly local needlecraft shop you could let them know what you are doing. For a small mention on your charity stall, the shop may be prepared to donate some fabrics and threads to your worthy cause. Ask for a few supplies at a time and I'm sure you will find plenty of shops that will cooperate with you. Also, to make sure as much as possible goes to charity, bulk buy your materials to save money over time.

483 A great way of raising funds for a charity is to have a swap shop with your likeminded stitching friends. Gather together all your unwanted kits, threads, fabric, charts etc and swap them between each other. Pay each other just a small amount for each thing swapped. You'll find the money soon adds up to a good sum, all for charity.

484 Use spare leftover threads and fabric to make small items to sell at a local craft fair or fête.

485 If you are stitching a wedding sampler, pick out a couple of motifs from the design – one to make a card, and another a gift tag – to give a completely coordinated gift.

486 If you finish a design for a special occasion, and it is going to be some time before you get it framed, store it carefully where it won't gather dirt and dust. Try a long cardboard tube.

487 **I don't have time to stitch large projects to give at Christmas – what small items can I stitch?**
You don't need to give huge designs as presents. Instead, choose small motifs and designs and, once stitched, mount them into quality accessories, such as trinket pots, paperweights, desk tidies and handbag mirrors.

488 If you are stitching a large quantity of the same design for wedding invitations or table settings, do all the stitching first, then mount the designs and then add any trimming you are using. Doing it this way will ensure that you do not run out of any materials halfway through.

489 **How do I choose a birth sampler to stitch when I don't know the sex of the baby that it is going to be for?**
Choose a design that will suit either a boy or girl, using lemon or mauve colours, and leave just the name to add after the baby's safe arrival.

490 When stitching a design for a wedding, try and find out the colour scheme for the day. You can then incorporate these colours into your design to make it more personal.

491 **What sort of gifts can I stitch and send through the post?** The only problem with sending gifts through the post is that framed pictures can be expensive to send and you run the risk of the glass being broken. To eliminate both these problems, go for lightweight gifts that aren't easily damaged. Bookmarks, tablelinen, coasters and bellpulls are all items that can be sent through the post. and they make great gifts. You should always make sure you use plenty of bubble wrap, or good protective packaging, to wrap a gift with before posting it, too. You should be safe then.

492 **How can I make a design look festive?** Make a design look festive by using festive colours for threads, such as reds and greens and sparkling blending filaments and metallic threads. You could also stitch designs on to red or green fabric to make them look seasonal. Also, try using something called Lurex aida. It is a special aida fabric with gold thread running through it, perfect for Christmas.

493 Stitching the cover kits from magazines is the perfect way to raise money for charity, especially if you only have a charity sale once a year. Save the kits from magazines to stitch and raise money.

494 How can I create some quick Christmas cards or gift tags?

Buy some navy aida or evenweave and stitch sparkling snowflakes on to the fabric using metallic threads. The designs will only take minutes to complete, but will look very effective and luxurious. You can make several of the same design very quickly.

495 What sort of designs are best to stitch for charity?

Choose designs that are quick and simple to do, so that you will be able to stitch lots to sell and really boost your fundraising. Try and pick designs that use just whole stitches and a small amount of backstitch. Cards do well on a stall selling for charity – everybody needs birthday cards and also cards for other occasions. Keyrings, bookmarks, coasters, napkin rings and fridge magnets all make ideal products for your stall.

496 Where can I sell my stitched items?

Ask a local gift shop if they will donate a small amount of space in their shop for you to sell your handstitched items for charity. Many charity shops will be more than happy to take stitched designs from you to sell. Alternatively, if you contact a charity they will give you details of fundraising events where you could perhaps hold a stall and sell your stitching.

497 Time is of the essence. Don't underestimate how much time you will need if stitching for something important like a wedding.

498 If you are stitching Christmas designs for charity, share skeins of specialist threads such as metallics, so that you don't spend unnecessarily on luxury items. Sparkly metallic threads come in a wide variety of colours and textures and are perfect for making a design look special, but they are expensive to buy.

499 If you want to stitch for birthdays and special occasions, keep a diary full of the important days and celebrations throughout the year that mean something to you. Write reminders in the diary a couple of months before the special event, so that you will have plenty of time to stitch your chosen design. You'll never miss an occasion, as long as you leave enough time for what you want to stitch, and you'll impress all your friends by never missing a special event!

500 **I'm stitching some small items for charity and want to do some fridge magnets. Is there an alternative to the ready-made plastic fridge magnets as they are expensive?** Try stitching your designs on plastic canvas, which doesn't need to be put into a plastic case. This canvas is much cheaper and comes in lots of different colours, and is also available clear. Once the stitching is complete, cut the canvas around the edge, one square away from the stitching. Oversew the edge all the way around and stick some card on the back. Attach a small self-adhesive magnet on the reverse side – perfect. Keyrings and coasters are also cheap alternatives to stitch.

501 Run a stitching competition – something like 'fastest stitcher'. You can even see if a local supermarket would be willing to donate a prize to the winner. If it gets a mention in the local paper it's publicity for your charity and for the supermarket too – everyone wins.

R

7.99

Please Quote erence: /124

NE

DIRECT Debit

ORDER FORM

☑ YES! I would like to subscribe to *The World of Cross Stitching* at just £7.99 per quarter by Direct Debit

Save over £11 throughout the year!

THE WORLD OF Cross Stitching

Direct Debit payment every quarter (UK only)

Instruction to your Bank or Building Society to pay by Direct Debit

DIRECT Debit origin

Please complete in ballpoint pen and send to *The World of Cross Stitching* subscriptions, Origin Publishing Ltd, Tower House, Sovereign Park, Market Harborough LE16 9EF

Name and full postal address of your Bank or Building Society

Name of Bank ______________________

Address ______________________

____

Postcode ______________________

Name(s) of account holders ______________________

Branch sort code ☐☐☐☐☐☐ Bank/Building Society ac/no ☐☐☐☐☐☐☐☐

Instruction to your Bank/Building Society

Please pay Origin Publishing Ltd Direct Debits from the account detailed in this instruction subject to the safeguards assured by the Direct Debit Guarantee. I understand that this instruction may remain with Origin Publishing Ltd and, if so, details will be passed electronically to my Bank/Building Society.

Signature(s) ______________________ Date __________

OFFICE USE ONLY

Originator's Identification Number

8	3	6	8	3	9

Reference Number: ☐☐☐☐☐☐☐☐☐☐

Banks and Building Societies may not accept Direct Debit instructions for some types of accounts

Your details

Mr/Mrs/Ms Name ______________________

Email address ______________________

Address ______________________

____

______________________ Postcode __________

Telephone number (in case of queries) ______________________

Please tick this box if you would like to receive information and offers from Origin Publishing Ltd. by: ☐email ☐SMS. Please tick this box if you would like to receive information and offers from selected companies by: ☐ email ☐SMS

Offer closes: 31 December 2004 Your subscription will start with the next available issue. Offer available to UK residents only.

We will use the details you have supplied to gain a better understanding of our magazine readership. If you DO NOT wish us to contact you about other products or services available from Origin Publishing, *please indicate here* ☐. *We may also pass your details onto other carefully selected companies whose products and services may be of interest to you. Please tick this box* ☐ *if you prefer NOT to receive such offers.*

W124

THE WORLD OF
Cross
Stitching